The Stock Market explains the instability and erratic movement of stock market prices. It describes and assesses theories of the determination of the level of and fluctuations in share prices. The practices of fund managers who now dominate activity on the stock market are analysed and related to Keynes's theories. Keynes's analysis of the stock market was at the heart of his explanation of economic instability and it is apt to reassess his theory at a time when economic instability is greater than at any time since the 1930s. The book provides a wealth of information about the operation of the stock market and returns on investments.

University of Cambridge
Department of Applied Economics

Occasional paper 59

The stock market

DAE Occasional papers

Earlier titles in this series and in the DAE Papers in Industrial Relations and Labour series may be obtained from:
The Publications Secretary, Department of Applied Economics, Sidgwick Avenue, Cambridge, CB3 9DE

The stock market

CLIFF PRATTEN

CAMBRIDGE
UNIVERSITY PRESS

Published by the Press Syndicate of the University of Cambridge
The Pitt Building, Trumpington Street, Cambridge CB2 1RP
40 West 20th Street, New York, NY 10011–4211, USA
10 Stamford Road, Oakleigh, Melbourne 3166, Australia

First published 1993

Printed in Great Britain at the University Press, Cambridge

A catalogue record for this book is available from the British Library

Library of Congress cataloguing in publication data

Pratten. C. F. (Clifford Frederick)
The Stock market / Cliff Pratten.
    p.   cm. – (DEA occasional papers)
Includes bibliographical references and index.
ISBN 0 521 44065 3
1. Stock-exchange. 2. Uncertainty. 3. Keynesian economics. I. Title.
II. Series: Occasional papers (University of Cambridge. Dept. of Applied Economics)
HG4551.P63 1993
332.64'2 – dc20 93–276 CIP

ISBN 0 521 440653 hardback

Contents

Illustrations

Figures

Boxes

Tables

Preface

I cannot claim to have made a £m by stock market investment even in shrunken 1990 £s. My record as an investor has been patchy, and both 1989 and 1990 were dismal years; in 1989 my shares failed to rise in line with the market and in 1990 some of them were hit very hard. This experience suggested the question: How have successful investors achieved their superior performance?

The study upon which the book is based did not originate to answer this question: rather, it grew out of inconclusive conversations with Tony Lawson which centred around the relevance of Keynes's writings about the stock market and the ways in which economic agents deal with uncertainty. Lawson's view is that uncertainty is pervasive, ruling out any significant knowledge of what shares are really worth, and that Keynes's analysis retains a good deal of relevance; I was not convinced. In the spring of 1990 we set out to clarify and resolve our debate by interviewing fund managers as a pilot for a project to study ways in which economic agents make decisions when faced with uncertainty. The main purpose of the interviews was to examine the procedures and practices of fund managers in order to test the contemporary relevance of Keynes's analysis.

With hindsight, it is clear that the summer of 1990 was an interesting time to interview fund managers. The stock market crash in October 1987 undermined the relevance of the theory underlying the 'Efficient Markets Hypothesis' which is described in chapter 2. In America, new analyses of the operation of the stock market were underway while this study was in preparation and were changing perceptions of the way markets operate. Both the eclipse of central planning and systematic privatisation in Britain and elsewhere had enhanced the role of stock markets and fund managers in allocating capital, and the political and economic background which affects the valuation of shares was eventful; according to opinion polls, the Conservative Government was unpopular and it faced an election within two years, the Iraq/Gulf crisis which started in August 1990 unsettled world stock markets, the

UK economy was moving into recession, the UK joined the Exchange Rate Mechanism (ERM) in October 1990 and there were various imbalances in the world economy.

Acknowledgements

I have benefited from a great deal of encouragement and advice in the preparation of this book. The study was started with Tony Lawson and together we drafted the questionnaire used at the interviews we arranged with fund managers. Unfortunately, Tony's many other commitments prevented him taking part in completing the study but he provided many helpful comments on the drafts and during discussions about the stock market.

Professor W. B. Reddaway read a draft of the book and provided a number of insights to the subject and many detailed comments. Professor Reddaway is better known to readers of the *Investors Chronicle* and of the *Financial Times* as 'Academic Investor'; his comments were based on practical experience of stock market investment as well as expertise as an economist. Jochen Runde and Peter Hutchinson took time out from their own studies to comment on drafts of the book. Stephen Pratten, Mark Lloyd, Simon Page and Probat Vaze assisted with preparation of the book.

Anne Mason and Sharon Swann prepared the typescript with their customary patience and efficiency, and Ann Newton provided skilful editorial assistance.

The contribution of fund managers is gratefully acknowledged; without their cooperation in answering the questionnaire the study would not have been possible.

Finally, and in this case most importantly, I have to absolve those who helped and assisted from the faults that remain. Although Tony Lawson, Brian Reddaway and Jochen Runde provided a great deal of help with the study, they would not take the same view as the author on *all* aspects of the subject. The book provides one author's view of Keynes's contribution to understanding the operation of the stock market and other theories, in particular the Efficient Markets Hypothesis, which have been developed to explain share prices.

CLIFF PRATTEN

October 1992

Introduction

The activities of buying and selling stocks and shares on the stock market are extremely important for the allocation of capital within economies. Although most of the business on the stock market consists of dealing in existing (secondary) securities, the prices of these securities provide important signals. Companies whose share prices are at a premium to the book value of their assets[1] and on low dividend yields have a 'badge of approval' which enhances their chances of borrowing capital on favourable terms and of raising capital by issuing new shares. Also, transaction prices and quotations provide investors with an indication of the market value of their wealth which may influence their decisions about consumption expenditure. When prices are at historically high levels and/or rising this indicates confidence among investors and may affect the confidence of businessmen and hence their investment decisions.

A brief description of the stock market

At the beginning of 1990 there were 29 market makers, firms which set prices at which they offer to trade shares, on the London Stock Exchange and shares of 2,400 UK and Irish companies were quoted. Shares of 179 of the companies were labelled alpha stocks and the median number of market makers for each of these stocks was 12 (the number of market makers for the stocks ranged from 4 to 18). There were 611 beta stocks and the median number of market makers was 5; for the 1,444 gamma stocks, the median number of market makers was 3. In addition to the market in UK equities, the London market deals in shares of companies based overseas, government stocks, bonds issued by UK-based and other companies, and options.

During the first quarter of 1990 daily turnover in UK (and Irish) equities on the Stock Exchange averaged £1,219m, equivalent to 0.2% of GDP; approximately one third of this turnover was intra-market (between market makers) and two-thirds was with other parties including institutions and individual investors – 'customer' business.[2] The number of customer bargains averaged 29,000 a day, and the average size of bargain was, oddly enough, about £29,000. In the first quarter of 1990 'customer' turnover represented 10% of the market capitalisation of equities (41% on an annual basis). As the turnover includes purchases and sales the implication is that 20% of shares are traded each year. In 1989 turnover was higher, implying that the equivalent of 30% of shares were traded that year.

The UK stock market has changed radically since the 1920s and 1930s, the period when Keynes was an active investor and obtained that experience of the market on which his writings about it were based. The changes include institutional changes and changes in the relative importance of categories of participants and market performance. It is outside the scope of this book to describe in detail the institutional changes which have been made since the 1930s, but among the most important were the relaxation of the rules governing investment by trustees introduced in the Trustee Investments Act 1961 and the increase in the number of market makers and the reduction in transaction costs for large deals associated with the 'Big Bang' changes in the London market made in 1986. Soon after Big Bang, screen-based trading replaced trading on the floor of the Stock Exchange: market makers and investors with access to screens can now call up the prices quoted by market makers for any stock. Other market innovations have included the introduction of new products such as traded options for a limited range of shares and forward contracts based on market indices. One purpose of the Big Bang changes was to make the UK market internationally competitive; international investment has always been important for UK companies and the City, but their relative importance has increased as restraints on the international flow of funds have been relaxed. Since 1979, UK residents have had freedom to transfer funds out of the UK and to sell sterling at the current exchange rate to invest in overseas assets.

Institutions

Through the post-Second World War period direct holdings of company securities by the public have diminished in relative importance. The share of UK equities held by the public in 1989 has been estimated at 18%, compared to 63% held by institutions.[3] In contrast, during the 1920s and 1930s more than two-thirds of the shares of companies with a stock market quotation were held by the public.[4] The development of institutions including the growth of pension funds, and the relaxation of rules governing investments by trustees, contributed to these changes. Another explanation for the reversal in holdings is the tax advantages enjoyed by institutional investors, insurance companies, pension funds, and investment and unit trusts. Also, people expect that professional fund managers will be able to outperform their own efforts – to add value in excess of the managers' fees less any value they impute to the time and effort they would have to devote to managing their own investments, and fund managers can invest in a more diversified portfolio to reduce risk than can a private investor with limited resources.

Aside from the regulatory changes and changes in the pattern of ownership, there have been changes in the role, importance, and perception of the stock market. Henry Kaufman (1986) has described these changes for American financial markets. He rightly suggests that the financial markets are more in the news and that the relative importance of financial markets has increased as the relative power of governments to manage economies has shrunk. In Britain the role of the stock market has been enhanced by the extensive programme of privatisation.

Plan of the book

The stock market is an enormous subject and no book can provide a comprehensive account of its operation. The initial purpose of the study reported here was to assess the contemporary relevance of Keynes's writings about the stock market, but, in order to place Keynes's writings in perspective, other theories of the determination of share prices are described in part I. Ownership of shares gives the owner rights to a flow of dividends from companies in the future. What a share is worth depends upon expectations about this flow of dividends, which depends upon numerous other factors including the profits of companies, which in turn depend upon the technical expertise and management of companies and the way the economy develops, relative to the expected returns on other assets. The problem underlying the valuation of shares is that profits and dividends cannot be predicted accurately more than two years ahead for most, if not all, companies – the rate of inflation, the buoyancy of the economy, the protection provided by patents and technical innovation change in unpredictable ways. For many companies, profits over a period as short as the next two years are difficult to forecast, and even the level of real profits for past periods may be obscure because of the treatment of inflation in the accounts resulting in the inclusion of stock appreciation in profits and inadequate allowance for the depreciation of capital equipment, and in some cases because of creative accounting. What any individual company's shares are *really worth* is unknowable. The uncertainty is somewhat less when forecasting the growth of aggregate dividends and assessing the total value of shares for the economy as a whole, since these are not much affected by the strategies adopted by the managements of individual companies, but the future rate of inflation and the rate of growth of the economy, which are important influences for aggregate profits and dividends, are uncertain.

Keynes's explanation for the volatility of share prices has at its heart the principle of uncertainty: it is not possible to pinpoint one price which a share is *really worth* or an index number which reflects the *real worth* of the market as a whole. Keynes argues that agents adopt various rules of thumb when faced with this uncertainty and traces the consequences for the instability of share prices. These theories are described in chapter 1.

No one denies that the future is uncertain, but some 'theorists' argue that investors predict the future in the sense that they act as if attaching probabilities to the various possible outcomes (including the possible future streams of dividends to be paid by companies), and act on these probability sets when investing. For these theorists, asset prices in the market reflect *fundamentals* – what shares are *really worth* – and changes in share prices are attributable to new information. The Efficient Markets Hypothesis (EMH) and related theories are described in chapter 2.

Chapter 3 examines other explanations, including other behavioural theories, for fluctuations in share prices. These are described, although I do not claim to have made much progress in measuring their importance, in order to place Keynes's views and the EMH in perspective and because they *could be* important for explaining some movements in share prices.

The second part of the book describes the investment markets and reports the returns on investments. In chapter 4 some characteristics of the stock market and share prices are reported. Chapters 5 and 6 examine two features of the performance of UK equities, the slow growth of real dividends and the undervaluation of equities *in the sense that the returns on investments in equities have been higher than returns on alternative investments*. In order to provide a benchmark for comparisons with the stock market, the market for commercial property is examined in chapter 7.

Part III of the book gives the results of the survey of fund managers. Chapter 8 describes the inquiry and the institutions included in the sample. Chapters 9 and 10 describe the procedures and methods which the fund managers of the sample of institutions use to allocate their funds to classes of investments and to pick shares. Chapter 11 considers the stock market from the viewpoint of market makers and fund managers' views of market making. There was a hundred-fold variation in the total funds managed by fund managers included in the sample and this variation suggested the question: How does differing size affect the competitiveness of institutions? This question is answered in chapter 12.

Part IV of the book reviews other evidence bearing on the operation of the stock market. As Keynes's views of the market are a focus of the study, his conduct and performance as an investor are the subject of chapter 13. Chapter 14 surveys the performance of fund managers, and the influence of the Press on share prices is considered in chapter 15.

The final part of the book provides a description of the results of the study: in chapter 16 the relevance of Keynes's analysis of the stock market and the EMH are assessed and the reasons for bubbles and bursts are considered, the general implications of the study are described in chapter 17, and an analysis of whether equities were still undervalued in September 1991 is reported in chapter 18.

Part I
Theory

1 Keynes's explanation for the instability of share prices and investment

The most readable and entertaining chapter of *The General Theory of Employment, Interest and Money* is chapter 12, 'The State of Long-term Expectations', in which Keynes analyses the operation of the stock market. Considerable debate nevertheless exists concerning its importance for Keynes's central contributions to economics. One purpose of the study which is reported in this book is somewhat at a tangent to these debates: it is to assess the present-day relevance of Keynes's description of the stock market. *The General Theory* was written in the aftermath of the 1929 stock market crash and the worldwide recession which followed it. The stock market crash of 1987, which was not immediately followed by a recession, and suggestions by some economists and politicians that 'short-termism' practised by investors has deleterious effects on the operation of the economy, have created topical interest in the workings of the Stock Exchange and Keynes's analysis of the determinants of stock market prices. In this chapter the arguments presented by Keynes in his chapter 12 are summarised in the light of recent interpretations and commentaries.[1]

Chapter 12 of *The General Theory*: the basic arguments

In chapter 12, Keynes attempts to explain the frequently experienced wide fluctuations in the volume of investment in commercial and industrial premises and machinery. For Keynes, the analysis of investment decisions must take into account the nature of uncertainty, the limits on the knowledge available to agents, and the institutional context in which entrepreneurs' expectations are formulated. Keynes distinguished between short-term and long-term expectations.[2] In theory, it is long-term expectations, the return expected to accrue as a result of producing with new capital equipment, which influence investment, and they are long-term because they extend as far into the future as the estimated life of the new acquisition.

Although an explanation for fluctuations in investment has to account for changes in expectations about returns from new investment projects, Keynes proceeded at one remove by concentrating on the way in which valuations of existing investments are carried out on the Stock Exchange.[3] Although the primary role of such valuations is to facilitate transfers of existing investments between agents rather than the financing of new investments in capital equipment, Keynes emphasised that they exert a significant influence on the rate of current investment. This follows from the fact that

> there is no sense in building up a new enterprise at a cost greater than that at which a similar existing enterprise can be purchased (or acquired by a takeover); while there is an inducement to spend on a new project what may seem to be an extravagant sum if it can be floated off on the Stock Exchange at an immediate profit. (CW, VII, p. 151)[4]

It is clear that, for Keynes, in order to uncover the roots of the problem of the periodic insufficiency and continual instability of investment, it is necessary to study the behaviour of stock market investors. As Keynes traces the source of the problem to the way in which existing investments are valued, the starting point is an examination of the process of valuing assets by investors. This part of Keynes's analysis has been side-stepped in most of the macroeconomic literature.

Conventions

Keynes suggests that valuations of existing investments are made on a conventional basis. These conventions were set out by Keynes in his 1937 *Quarterly Journal of Economics (QJE)* article, 'The General Theory of Employment' which describes 'the main grounds' for his departure from orthodox theory. There he suggested that agents adopt certain conventions or 'rules of thumb'; they

> 1 assume that the present is a much more serviceable guide to the future than a candid examination of past experience would show it to have been hitherto. In other words (agents) largely ignore the prospect of future changes about the actual character of which we know nothing.
> 2 ... assume that the existing state of opinion as expressed in prices and the character of existing output is based on a correct summing up of future prospects so that (agents) can accept it as such unless and until something new and relevant comes into the picture.
> 3 ... knowing [their] individual judgement is worthless ... [they] endeavour to fall back on the judgement of the rest of the world which is perhaps better informed. That is, [they] endeavour to conform with the behaviour of the majority or the average. The psychology of a society of individuals each of whom is endeavouring to copy others leads to what we may strictly term a *conventional* judgement. (CW, XIV, p. 114).

According to Keynes, the application of conventions can give rise to highly unstable – precarious – and arbitrary states, particularly so as the existing market evaluation cannot be uniquely correct given limitations of knowledge. 'In point of fact all sorts of considerations enter into the market valuation which are in no way relevant to the prospective yield' (CW, VII, p. 152). Consequently, '. . . it is not surprising that a convention, in an absolute view of things so arbitrary, should have its weak points. It is its precariousness which creates no small part of our contemporary problem of securing sufficient investment' (CW, VII, p. 153). Keynes elaborates on this point in the *QJE* article:

> . . . a practical theory of the future based on these three principles has certain marked characteristics. In particular, being based on so flimsy a foundation, it is subject to sudden and violent changes. The practice of calmness and immobility, of certainty and security suddenly breaks down. New fears and hopes will without warning take charge of human conduct. The forces of disillusion may suddenly impose a new conventional basis of valuation. (CW, XIV, p. 114–15)

Uncertainty

Keynes's discussion of conventions is tied to his analysis of uncertainty, and in order to appreciate his views on the valuation of shares it is necessary to examine his treatment of uncertainty.[5] Keynes argues that the task of forecasting yields is next to, if not impossible. He writes:

> The outstanding fact is the extreme precariousness of the basis of knowledge on which our estimates of future yield have to be made . . . If we speak frankly we have to admit that our basis of knowledge for estimating the yield ten years hence of a railway . . . the goodwill of a patent medicine . . . a building in the City of London, amount to little and sometimes to nothing. (CW, VII, p. 149–50)[6]

Moreover, when criticising the view of 'classical economists', Keynes emphases that uncertainty cannot be reduced to, or tamed via, the calculus of probability, as is shown most clearly in the *QJE* paper of 1937:

> By uncertain knowledge, let me explain, I do not mean merely to distinguish what is known for certain from what is only probable. The game of roulette is not subject, in this sense to uncertainty; nor is the prospect of a Victory bond being drawn. Or again, the expectation of life is only slightly uncertain . . . The sense in which I am using the term is that in which the prospect of a European war is uncertain, or the price of copper and the rate of interest twenty years hence, or the obsolescence of a new invention or the position of private wealth owners in the social system in 1970. About these matters there is no scientific basis on which to form any calculable probability whatever. We simply do not know. (CW, XIV, p. 113–14)

Keynes's account of uncertainty is associated with the absence of probabilistic knowledge. It would appear that, for Keynes, uncertainty corresponds to a situation in which probabilities are not determinate or even comparable. Keynes's view of probability, which underlies his conception of uncertainty, harks back to his earliest work *A Treatise on Probability*: 'By saying that not all probabilities are measurable, I mean that it is not possible to say of every pair of conclusions, about which we have some knowledge, that the degree of our rational belief in one bears any numerical relation to the degree of our rational belief in the other ...' (CW, VIII, p. 37). For Keynes, probability arises out of a logical relation between propositions. Keynes's conception of probability can be clarified by contrasting it with the views of the 'frequentists' on the one hand and the 'subjectivists' on the other. A frequentist regards probability as a stable relative frequency of some kind of event in repeated trials. On this view, probability is a property of things or processes in the world. Keynes objected to this conception of probability, suggesting that it restricts the range of probability reasoning to an unduly narrow range of decision making. Meanwhile the subjectivists, like Keynes, see probabilities as a degree of belief that may be attached to any proposition or event. The difference between Keynes and the subjectivists is that for Keynes, probability relations are objective in that they reflect the degree of belief it is rational to hold in any given situation, while for subjectivists, probabilistic knowledge does not necessarily correspond to anything in external reality.[7]

Given the nature of the uncertainty investors face, what rational basis (see Box 1 for a definition of rationality) remains for them to carry out valuations of existing investments? In attempting to answer this question, Keynes asserts that when the information that is sought after is unavailable, it is rational to fall back on any relevant knowledge that is available, even if it is less directly relevant to the object at hand. As he puts it:

> It would be foolish, in forming our expectations to attach great weight to matters which are very uncertain. It is reasonable, therefore, to be guided to a considerable degree by the facts about which we feel somewhat confident, even though they may be less decisively relevant to the issue than other facts about which our knowledge is vague and scanty. For this reason the facts of the existing situation enter in a sense disproportionately, into the formation of our long term expectations; our usual practice being to take the existing situation and to project it into the future, modified only to the extent that we have more or less definite reasons for expecting a change. (CW, VII, p. 148)

This quotation relates to the first of the conventional practices which Keynes was later to identify in the *QJE* article noted above – 'that the present is a much more serviceable guide to the future than a candid examination of past experience would show it to have been hitherto'.

Box 1   Rational behaviour

The subject of rationality is extremely broad and complex.* The terms 'rational' and 'irrational' behaviour are open to many interpretations. Following Vercelli (1991), it is useful to distinguish between 'adaptive' rationality, where it is assumed that an agent cannot modify the alternative options available – either directly or indirectly by affecting the structure of the economy – and 'creative' rationality which acknowledges the human capacity consciously to modify the environment.

Adaptive rationality has itself to be considered from the perspective of 'substantive' rationality and 'procedural' rationality. Substantive rationality considers behaviour in an equilibrium context and refers to the attributes of the equilibrium configuration. It is assumed that the reality under examination is characterised by an optimal equilibrium given certain aims and circumstances, and it is assumed that only this equilibrium is scientifically relevant. One justification often put forward for this procedure is that any other position would only be transitory, as it would imply the existence of over-looked opportunities that would sooner or later be discovered and exploited by agents acting in their own interest. The influence of substantive rationality can be traced in all accounts which ignore the existence of bounds to human rationality.

Procedural rationality, meanwhile, refers to attributes of the dynamic process seen in all its dimensions (including disequilibrium). According to Simon (1982), behaviour is procedurally rational when it is the outcome of appropriate deliberation. Thus procedural rationality depends on the process that generated it and this process is often interpreted as a process of learning or movement towards equilibrium.

However, both these variants of adaptive rationality, substantive and procedural rationality, ignore an essential aspect of rationality, namely creative rationality, behaviour aimed at modifying the circumstances in which an agent operates.

Turning to Keynes, it is only rarely that he mentions cases of obvious irrationality. However, Keynes's conception of rational behaviour has little to do with the substantive form which dominates in economic and financial theory today. What matters for Keynes is that agents exercise judgement in particular situations and that they have reasons for acting as they do. Keynes's views can thus be seen as being more in line with procedural rationality, while his general framework could be seen as consistent with creative rationality.

It follows that the term irrational behaviour is much more precisely defined by economists than just 'contrary to or not in accord with reason'. The possible impact of irrational behaviour is considered in chapter 3.

* For a summary of the relevant debates the reader is referred to Sen (1987) and Vercelli (1991) and, for discussions of Keynes's conception of rational behaviour, to Runde (1991) and Lawson (1991).

As Runde (1991) has pointed out, this conventional practice carries with it the implication that agents accept that prices 'correctly' sum up the existing state of opinion about future prospects (the second of the conventional practices identified in the *QJE* article). Agents treat, *and suppose that other agents will treat* the existing set of market valuations, however formed, as though they are correct in relation to existing knowledge of the facts which influence the yield on investment and that they will only change in proportion to changes in this knowledge. Despite the fact that 'all sorts of considerations enter the market valuation which are in no way relevant to the prospective yield' (CW, VII, p. 152), this type of behaviour by investors can give rise to a certain degree of stability, as Keynes notes:

> the above conventional method of calculation will be compatible with a considerable measure of continuity and stability in our affairs, *so long as we can rely on the maintenance of the convention.*
>
> For if there exist organised investment markets and if we can rely on the maintenance of the convention, an investor can legitimately encourage himself with the idea that the only risk he runs is that of a genuine change in the news over the near future, as to the likelihood of which he can attempt to form his own judgement and which is unlikely to be very large. (CW, VII, p. 152–3)

Keynes seems to be implying that the conventional basis for the behaviour of investors may give rise to considerable stability, whereas, as mentioned earlier, the aim of his chapter is to explain wide fluctuations in investment. It is clear, however, that these two assertions in chapter 12 do not contradict one another, when it is remembered that the conventional basis of investors' behaviour operates in a setting of thorough-going uncertainty. It is this and not a reliance on conventions *per se* that renders the situation precarious and intermittently volatile. Since market valuations at any point in time cannot be based on a significant knowledge of eventual yields (for this does not exist) and because at any time there may be changes in relevant news, the situation, though perhaps often stable, will simultaneously be highly precarious – a perceived potential for change due to the possible arrival of 'news' will be present. Thus the existing conventional valuation may at some moment give way and the 'forces of disillusion may suddenly impose a new conventional basis of valuation' (CW, XIV, p. 115).

Keynes notes that this precariousness is heightened with the increase in the proportion of those people owning equities who are ignorant with respect to the prospects of the investment in question. Keynes writes:

> A conventional valuation which is established as the outcome of the mass psychology of a large number of ignorant individuals is liable to change violently as the result of a sudden fluctuation of opinion due to factors which

do not really make much difference to the prospective yield; since there will be no strong roots of conviction to hold it steady. (CW, VII, p. 154)

According to Keynes, the factors which exacerbate the fragility and precariousness of the market will not be counteracted by competition between expert professionals possessing judgement and knowledge beyond that of the average private investor. For most of these people are not concerned with what Keynes calls enterprise, i.e. the activity of forecasting the prospective yield of assets over their whole life, but with speculation, the activity of forecasting the psychology of the market. While from the standpoint of society speculative activity could be seen as damaging, from the standpoint of the investor it is quite justifiable: 'For it is not sensible to pay 25 for an investment of which you believe the prospective yield to justify a value of 30, if you also believe that the market will value it at 20 three months hence' (CW, VII, p. 155).[8]

Once the calm has been disturbed, how is stability restored? A clue is provided by Keynes's discussion of professional investors who are attempting to anticipate the basis of conventional valuation a short while ahead. Keynes famously likens such activity to a newspaper competition in which competitors are attempting to choose the prettiest face from a group of photographs when they know that the winning choice will be that which most nearly corresponds to the average preferences of the competitors as a whole. Here

> it is not a case of choosing those which, to the best of one's judgement, are really the prettiest, nor even those which average opinion genuinely thinks the prettiest. We have reached the third degree where we devote our intelligences to anticipating what average opinion expects average opinion to be. And there are some, I believe, who practise the fourth, fifth and higher degrees. (CW, VII, p. 156)

Thus, once stability has been lost, all that can be inferred in advance is that the new conventional evaluation will be one outcome from a large number of possibilities and that it will be precarious.

There is a two-way relationship between uncertainty and instability in financial markets: uncertainty leads to precarious prices because it makes for difficulty in estimating what shares are really worth, and volatile prices increase uncertainty about actual prices in the future.

Such considerations led Keynes to toy with ideas for reforming the Stock Exchange. Perhaps, 'in the public interest', it should be made 'inaccessible and expensive', possibly through the taxation of transactions or, more radically, by making the purchase of an investment permanent and indissoluble. There was a dilemma, however: while on the one hand the liquidity offered by the stock market might help promote instability, on the other hand it made individuals more willing to run the risks of new investment.

Keynes's propositions to be examined

Keynes's account of the operation of the stock market was conden-sed, which makes it difficult to identify his key propositions. Nonethe-less, the following list of propositions is suggested by a reading of chapter 12 and the *QJE* article:

1   it is difficult or impossible to forecast long-term yields on many investments;

2   investors assume the current state of affairs will continue indefinitely except in so far as there are definite reasons for expecting a change (Convention 1);

3   investors assume that existing market prices are based on a correct summing up of future prospects (Convention 2);

4   investors endeavour to conform with the behaviour of the majority or average (Convention 3);

5   professional investors are preoccupied with foreseeing changes in the conventional basis of valuation a short time ahead of the general public, not with making superior long-term forecasts of the probable yields of investments;

6   reliance on conventions when taking decisions affected by uncertainty can impart stability as opposed to volatile prices at times, but the stability is precarious, and at other times reliance upon conventions leads to instability – especially when circumstances change;

7   the instability of the market will increase as the proportion of shares owned by ignorant individuals (unprofessional investors) increases. However, the practices of professional investors, treating the market like a beauty contest, leads to instability if the conventional basis of valuation is disturbed.

2 The Efficient Markets Hypothesis

Since the publication of *The General Theory* in 1936 a separate academic discipline has emerged which addresses itself specifically to financial issues. Tobin (1984) has described finance theory as 'a burgeoning activity in academia, occupying more and more faculty slots, student credit hours, journal pages and computer printouts both in management schools and in economics departments'. In this chapter the explanations of asset price determination which have been developed within this literature are summarised. The Efficient Markets Hypothesis (EMH) and the debates surrounding it constitute a useful focus for this discussion.

The EMH – an outline

At its most general level the theory of efficient capital markets is the theory of competitive equilibrium applied to asset markets. Within this framework, a capital market is seen as being efficient if it utilises all the available information in setting the prices of assets. Prices of securities are determined by the conditions of equilibrium in competitive markets populated by self-interested rational agents. (Rationality here relates to substantive form rationality, described in Box 1.) Individual traders take positions in assets in response to the information available to them and according to their personal financial situations. The market aggregates this information and it is in this sense that it reflects the available information. Thus information that is universally available cannot provide the basis for profitable trading rules. For example, if it is generally known that a firm has favourable earnings prospects, the theory of efficient capital markets says that the price of that firm's stock will be bid to the point where no extra-normal capital gain on the stock will occur when the high earnings materialise. Therefore, knowledge that earnings will rise in the future does not imply that the stock should be bought now: it is only differences in information – information that is not 'fully-reflected' in prices – that can form the basis for profitable trading rules.

Box 2   Fundamentals

Fundamentals have been defined as 'the basic parameters defining an economy – such as endowments, preferences and production possibilities' (Cass and Shell, 1983). Fundamentals can be contrasted with extrinsic influences such as changes in animal spirits and market psychology. The 'fundamental' value of an asset is the present value of the expected future returns from the asset. The problem of determining the fundamental value of an asset which is to be held for an extended period of time consists of three parts: first, the problem of estimating the income to be received over time; second, the problem of estimating the terminal value the asset will have at the end of the period; and third, the problem of deciding upon a discount rate to be used for translating future returns into current values.

For equity investments, the EMH implies that investors can forecast returns – that they estimate a probability distribution for each company's profits and dividends for each year stretching into the distant future.

The account of the EMH given in this chapter highlights the connections between this hypothesis and particular notions of rationality, equilibrium and the analysis of information and uncertainty. In order to disentangle these elements, a historical sketch of the emergence of the EMH is provided. Although the underpinning of the EMH is vital to an understanding of theoretical analysis of the operation of the stock market, readers not concerned with this theory could pass to the section describing Fama's definition of the EMH on p. 23, after noting the contents of Box 2.

Fundamentals, 'fundamental analysis' and random walkers

Early works dealing with securities analysis (such as Graham and Dodd, 1934) put forward the idea that the 'intrinsic' or 'fundamental' value of any security equals the discounted cash flow which that security gives title to, and that actual prices fluctuate around these fundamental values. Accordingly, financial analysts were instructed to recommend buying (selling) securities that were priced below (above) fundamental values and to realise profits when the disparities were eliminated. Since little practical guidance was given concerning the discount rate to use, fundamental analysis in practice consisted of forming projections of future cash flow. This involved analysing the demand for the product made by a firm, the possible future development of substitutes, changes in the regulatory environment, etc. – in short, all information relevant to future profitability.

LeRoy (1989) notes that as early as 1933 empirical evidence emerged which did not support fundamental analysis. Alfred Cowles (1933) demonstrated that the recommendations of major brokerage houses, presumably based at least partly on fundamental analysis, did not outperform the market. The implication was that investors who paid for these recommendations were wasting their money. In 1934, Holbrook Working argued that 'random walks' characteristically developed patterns that look like those commonly ascribed by market analysts to stock prices. Was it possible that the model which provided the 'best' description of the time path of any particular stock predicted that in any future period the price would be equal to the price of that same security in the immediately preceding period, plus some totally random increment? Studies by Kendall (1953) and Granger and Morgenstern (1963) supported the random walk hypothesis.

These empirical observations raised an awkward question for the proponents of fundamental analysis. If fundamental analysis worked, why did not new entrants into the business of fundamental analysis, realising this fact, compete trading gains away? That is what is supposed to occur in other competitive industries, so why not in financial markets? The random walk results suggested that, in fact, this is exactly what did happen.

At first, the random walk model seemed to contradict not only the received orthodoxy of fundamental analysis, but also the very idea of rational securities pricing. The random walk model seemed to imply that stock prices are exempt from the laws of supply and demand that determine other prices. However, Harry Roberts (1964) pointed out that, in the economists' idealised market of rational individuals, one would expect exactly the instantaneous adjustment of prices to new information that the random walk model implies if the new information came as totally random increments. A pattern of systematic slow adjustment to new information, on the other hand, would imply the existence of readily available and profitable opportunities that were not being exploited.[1]

The random walk model was a far from complete explanation of asset price determination and, in fact, lacked internal consistency. The random walkers expected one to believe:

> 1 that unexploited patterns in securities prices cannot persist because for them to do so would imply that investors are irrationally passing up profit opportunities, but also
> 2 that investors are nonetheless irrationally wasting their money year after year employing useless securities analysts.
> If the argument that no behaviour inconsistent with rationality and rational expectations can persist in equilibrium is employed it must be employed consistently and this the random walkers were not doing. (LeRoy, 1989, p. 1588)

Up to this point, what may be called the pre-history of efficient capital markets has been described. The modern literature can be seen as starting with Samuelson's (1965) paper and, in particular, Fama's (1970) survey article. However, to appreciate this modern literature it is necessary to place it in the context of developments in economic theorising more generally.

When discussing the contemporary theory of financial markets it is particularly important to recognise the connection between this theory and, firstly, the notion of equilibrium, specifically as it is expressed in neo-Walrasian models of generalised market equilibrium and, secondly, the related treatment of uncertainty. For readers not familiar with these elements of economic theory they are outlined in the next section. Theorists themselves accept that there are still serious qualifications/flaws to the models outlined below, as representations of actual economies.

Equilibrium and uncertainty

Walras was the first to point out that there is no obvious reason to expect identity between the prices yielded by the solution of his system of demand and supply equations and the prices which would, in fact, emerge in a freely competitive market. He therefore developed his theory of *tâtonnement* in which he envisioned a market where people appear with inventories of various goods as well as with well-defined marginal utility functions. Walras suggested that equilibrium could be brought about by means of the successive announcement of provisional prices; if the demands and offers called forth by the announcement of a price did not balance, then fresh prices would be proposed. This process of trial and error, pricing and re-pricing, then continues until, according to Walras, the actual market prices converge to those which equate supply and demand. It has been pointed out that a necessary part of this process must be Edgeworth's recontracting device. The quantities supplied and demanded at tentative interim prices must themselves constitute only provisional commitments, so that if prices change all offers to buy and sell can be reversed completely. For unless buyers and sellers were permitted to change their minds as prices were modified, the set of prices finally determined by the *tâtonnement* process would depend on the nature of the randomly selected initial prices. People who had readily committed themselves and their purchasing power heavily at an early stage would not be able to take advantage of the revised price pattern which emerged out of the process.

General Equilibrium Theory traditionally involves the assumption of a Walrasian *tâtonnement* equilibrating process and the generally accompanying postulate of Edgeworth-type recontracting in tentative market confrontations.

It is these same equilibrating processes which are involved in much modern financial markets theory, and this means that the assumption that no transactions are binding at non-equilibrium prices is ensconced also in the theoretical analysis of financial asset pricing and capital markets. Fama and Miller, for example, have embedded their discussion of financial market equilibrium on the assumption that

> prices and decisions are tentative, because it is agreed that no decisions will be executed until an equilibrium set of prices, that is, a set of prices at which all markets can clear at period 1, has been determined. Our treatment of this model ... concentrates on the nature of equilibrium in the capital market. (Fama and Miller, 1972, p. 150)

Walras himself considered the stock market to be the market which most closely approximated his *tâtonnement* process. He wrote: 'The particular groping which we have just described actually takes place in the stock exchange' (Walras, 1954, p. 289). Despite this quotation, it is quite clear that the *tâtonnement* mechanism is far removed from the pricing of shares on the stock market. As Baumol points out,

> we know this is not how things work out in practice. Except, perhaps, in some auction markets people generally do not make tentative bids nor are prices usually determined by a trial and error process. Such a procedure would be extremely difficult to administer and to keep track of, especially with the large number of participants necessary to render a market competitive in the sense used in economic theory. (Baumol, 1965, p. 11)

Baumol notes that in practice stock exchanges deal with large numbers of buyers and sellers by operating in a manner somewhat analogous to a representative democracy: the various bidders make their desires known through a much smaller number of brokers who represent them. Moreover, offers to sell and purchase are not collected up and made to correspond with one another simultaneously. Bids arrive either sporadically or continuously throughout the trading day; pricing is thus a dynamic process.

Turning to the treatment of uncertainty, it is generally agreed that in a world of 'certainty', asset markets such as the stock market would have little reason to exist. Any understanding of such markets depends upon the introduction of uncertainty.

Debreu (1959) represents a useful starting point for an outline of the conventional approach to the economics of uncertainty. In his work on the theory of value, which extended the Walrasian framework and placed it on a new footing, Debreu considered the case where the character of the consumption and production sets and the resource availabilities in the economy are determinable by uncertain events. From the foundation which Debreu provided, a theory of time–state preferences has developed in which (usually complete) markets are assumed to exist for claims on future dated commodities whose availability is contingent on the occurrence of specifiable future states or events. Here, in the absence of uncertainty, every commodity is specified by its physical characteristics and by the location and date of its availability. Uncertainty is introduced by specifying commodities not only by their standard characteristics but also by the environmental context or 'state of nature'. A commodity is considered to be quite different where two different environmental contexts have been realised. This by no means exhausts the possible ways of treating uncertainty and, in fact, differs radically from Keynes's approach to uncertainty (outlined in chapter 1).

The standard treatment proceeds by discussing the equilibrium configuration in an environment where there is a complete set of contingent markets. (Within this framework a system of markets is said to be complete when every contingency at every available future time corresponds to a distinct marketable commodity or claim.) Prices set in such markets would clear supplies and demands in advance for all such commodities, with each participant constrained by his budget to promise no more than he or she could deliver. This 'benchmark' system would realise the claims for the economy-wide efficiency and optimality of competitive markets. Following this, the case of 'missing' or 'incomplete' markets (i.e. the situation where markets for some conceivable time–space claims do not exist) is investigated, and it is at this point that markets such as the stock market are incorporated into the analysis. It can be shown that securities and insurance markets can mimic the system associated with complete contingent markets provided that the menu of available securities 'spans' all the 'states of nature' (that is, there must be as many different independent securities as there are conceivable time–space claims). Actual financial institutions fall short of this vision. There are good reasons for this. Markets require resources to operate and, given their costs, particularly when assets have diverse characteristics, it would be inefficient to have a complete set of markets.

More recently, the incorporation of rational expectations equilibrium has opened up new theoretical perspectives regarding the stock market.[2] One branch of this recent theoretical work suggests that asset prices may have an additional informational role (above and beyond their conventional role in determining budget sets for consumers and profit opportunities for firms).[3] Traders have information which affects their evaluation of the value of assets, the demand for the assets and thus prices. Other traders may attempt to infer the information from prices.[4] According to Bray (1989), the major achievement of this recent literature has been to develop a coherent description of this role of prices and to use it to ask how well the markets transmit and aggregate the information.

The emergence of the Efficient Markets Hypothesis

Samuelson's (1965) paper was of importance for the emergence of the modern literature concerning the EMH. Unlike the random walk approach, Samuelson's analysis with its characterisation of equilibrium using a martingale model constituted an economic model of asset price determination that could be linked with traditional assumptions about preferences and returns. (A price follows a martingale process if on average it remains stable – that is, it varies randomly about a constant mean.) LeRoy suggests that it is best to view the martingale model as an extreme version of the fundamental model modified by assuming that a large majority of traders are conducting fundamental analyses, are arriving at the same estimates of fundamental values, and are trading appropriately; thus price will be bid to equality with fundamental value and opportunities for trading profits will disappear. 'Instead of assuming that price fluctuates around fundamental value, Samuelson assumed ... that price actually equals fundamental value' (LeRoy, 1989, p. 1591). This viewpoint is in marked contrast to Keynes's perceptions of the difficulty/impossibility of assessing the real value of many assets and the importance of extrinsic influences on asset prices.

Fama's (1970) survey marks the start of the modern literature on efficient capital markets. Fama's paper, like the material it surveyed, was largely concerned with empirical work. However, Fama also provided some preliminary theoretical discussion and these theoretical remarks (together with his 1970 contribution) were influential in the sense of determining the nature of the work which followed. Fama utilised the martingale model and it should be stressed that by doing so he identified market efficiency with the validity of a particular model of equilibrium in financial markets. Market efficiency thus becomes a complex joint hypothesis.

Fama's three versions of the EMH

In Fama's discussion, a capital market is efficient if all the available information is fully reflected in security prices.[5] Fama then distinguished three versions of the efficient markets model depending on the specification of the information set. At one end of the spectrum is strong-form efficiency. Strong-form efficiency asserts that the information set used by the market to set prices contains all of the available information that could possibly be relevant to pricing the asset. Not only is all *publicly available* information embodied in the price but all privately held information is as well. A substantial notch down from strong-form efficiency is semi-strong-form efficiency. A market is efficient in the semi-strong sense if it uses all of the publicly available information. The important distinction is that the information set is not assumed to include privately held information.[6] At the bottom of the ladder in the efficiency hierarchy is weak-form efficiency which requires only that the current and past price history be incorporated in the information set.

Tests of the EMH

The EMH asserts that asset prices reflect fundamental values of the assets which were defined in Box 2. Econometricians testing the application of the theory to share prices face a dilemma – ideally, they would test whether prices do reflect fundamental values, but they have no measure of these values because the future returns on the assets are uncertain. They cannot provide direct tests of the theory and have to use a proxy for fundamental values or test whether the characteristics of stock market prices or the performance of portfolios are consistent with the theory.

The weak form of the EMH has been exhaustively tested and some qualifications to its application have been established. The tests, most of which have been based on US data, take the form of specifying a rule which conflicts with the EMH and testing for the application of the rule; for example, tests have been carried out to see if the sequence of daily gains and losses is random by attempting to use the actual sequence of gains and losses to predict future gains or losses. If prices of shares rise for, say, two consecutive days are they more likely to rise than fall on the third day? Until recently such simple tests have usually failed to contravene the EMH, but some flaws have been established; for example:

1   there is some evidence that the shares of small firms have outperformed the market over long, but not all, periods;
2   companies with low P/E ratios have scored above average returns (a P/E ratio is the ratio of the price of a company's shares to the company's earnings per share for the latest year for which this information is available);
3   movements in the US stock market are disproportionately concentrated in January;
4   the existence of and/or predictable changes in the discount of the

prices of shares in investment trusts to the stock market valuation of the portfolios of shares held by the investment trusts conflicts with the EMH.

The 1987 Crash, when the Dow Jones index fell by 30.7% in six days, gave a new impetus and direction to tests of the EMH and added credibility to tests which contradicted the hypothesis; because such a *large* and *swift* fall was not compatible with changes in stock market prices being determined by new information concerning fundamentals alone. Prior to 1987, Shiller (1981) had apparently punctured the EMH by demonstrating that, historically, share prices had fluctuated much more than the discounted flow of dividends; fluctuations in share prices had occurred which could not be explained by fundamentals. (The tests used by Shiller are outlined in chapter 4.) Recently, more penetrating statistical tests have been used to test the EMH and have shown that 'stock returns exhibit positive serial correlation over short periods and negative correlation over longer intervals' (Poterba and Summers, 1987). The novelty of the new tests is that they are used to test for positive and negative correlations over protracted periods. On a day-to-day basis price changes may appear to be random or nearly so, but over a period of say 50 years there may be a persistent element in price changes. To test for such patterns, data for long periods of time are required and/or data for a number of stock markets.

Tests have been made of the semi-strong form of the EMH by examining how quickly new information is reflected in prices – market efficiency requires that it is reflected rapidly and that investors cannot achieve above-average returns by studying, say, the annual results of companies a week after they are published. Again, only limited deviations from the EMH have been established and Fama (1991) attaches considerable significance to these results; he suggests that they 'give the most direct evidence on market efficiency'. In fact, there is an important qualification to this conclusion. All that the results show is that the market does not rapidly change its view of the significance of news, which is very different from saying that it assesses the long-term implications of news accurately.

The strong form of the EMH is not susceptible to testing because there is no way of knowing the information available to all the participants in the market including, for example, the directors of companies and others who have inside information, and the use they make of this information as investors.

The EMH supposition that the market fully and correctly reflects all relevant information in determining security prices is at odds with the fact that different investors simultaneously hold different expectations for future movements of share prices (McInish and Srivastava, 1984). The heavy turnover of shares which involves willing buyers and sellers is also witness to different assessments of value, though some exponents of the EMH would argue that the turnover of shares by institutions is excessive.

Although breaches have been opened in the EMH, it is not clear that the flaws identified enable investors to adopt a *rule* which makes it possible for them to outperform the market, because they would incur transaction costs which would offset part or all of the gains. Also, if a profitable rule were discovered, publication of the rule would be likely to lead market makers and market participants to move to eliminate the opportunity. (There could be an initial phase when as a result of many investors applying the rule there were exaggerated movements of share prices.)

A notable feature of many of the statistical tests of the EMH is that the rules tested are very simple, much simpler than the procedures which are used by institutional investors to allocate funds between classes of investments and to select shares, and which are described later in this book. (This observation does not apply to tests based on a comparison of the performance of fund managers.) Also, random lapses from efficient use of information, even if they are widespread and pervasive, may not be exposed by tests for market failure which aim to expose systematic failure.

Conclusions and suggested questions

This review of the Efficient Capital Markets literature has high-lighted the assumptions upon which the theory has been based, such as a concentration on equilibrium states and a particular treatment of uncertainty. It has been suggested that the stress on equilibrium states is problematic, since pricing on the stock market necessarily consti-tutes a dynamic process, and that the treatment of uncertainty under-lying the theoretical formulation of the EMH represents only one possible account of uncertainty and not necessarily the most adequate. A number of possible strategies for further work suggest themselves from this discussion. At a very basic level one could reassess the methodological and theoretical underpinnings of this literature – this would involve, for example, questioning the status of such notions as equilibrium, examining the conceptualisation of 'rational behaviour' and analysing in depth the treatment of uncertainty. Another strategy would involve examining in detail the quantitative analyses which relate to the EMH and assessing the extent to which such work can be said to 'test' the EMH. A third possible strategy, and the one adopted here, is to use simple quantitative techniques to refocus attention on the stock market as such and thereby avoid becoming constrained and side-tracked by the considerable, supposedly supportive, mathematical apparatus which accompanies modern treatments of the stock market.

Questions

1 In the first two chapters, two sets of forces determining stock market prices were identified – 'fundamentals' and 'others'. Which of these two sets of forces is relatively the more important? According to the EMH, fundamentals alone determine share prices.

2 The EMH incorporates equilibrium conditions and strict assumptions regarding investor behaviour. Are the procedures adopted by investors compatible with these assumptions?

3 The EMH predicts that investors cannot consistently outperform the index; so one obvious question is: Do some investors consistently outperform the index? However, even if it could be shown that no investors consistently outperformed the index, this would not confirm the EMH because the failure of investors to consistently outperform the index is also compatible with the view that no one can predict the future.

4 If some investors do consistently outperform the index, how is this performance achieved? Is inside knowledge the explanation or does their record conflict with the weaker forms of the EMH?

3 Other explanations for the volatility of share prices

Keynes's analysis provides an explanation for the volatility of share prices in terms of uncertainty and conventions. Within the EMH schema, share prices reflect fundamentals and the explanation for fluctuations in share prices is that new events and information change the expected returns from assets and hence share prices.

Unexpected changes in monetary conditions are new events which can have an important influence on share prices; for example, a reduction in interest rates which was not expected by investors would reduce the discount rate for calculating the present value of the future stream of dividends from equities and lead to increases in share prices; the prices of shares move in sympathy with changes in interest rates to maintain the relationships between the expected future stream of dividends on equities and the expected returns on deposits and bonds. Previously, controls on lending may have limited borrowing to finance the acquisition of assets, and relaxation of controls may increase demand for assets including equities. An effective relaxation of controls on bank lending is likely to raise asset prices and could result in bankers and others misreading price signals and in over-lending by banks and over-trading by their customers. Increased competition among lenders could lead to customers gearing up their operations and taking greater risks, and hence to more defaults. Also, a splurge of lending following deregulation could have echo effects – a credit shortage could follow as and when banks reach new limits on their lending or are hit by bad debts (Kaufman, 1986; Davis, 1990). An unexpected reduction in interest rates or a relaxation of credit controls may lead to an expectation of faster inflation, increased output, higher profits and share prices, and so again increase demand for equities.

Recently, some theorists, while not wishing to abandon the assumptions on which the EMH is based, have acknowledged that the case for

---

Box 3   Bubbles

Kindleberger has defined bubbles as 'a sharp rise in the price of an asset
. . . in a continuous process, with the initial rise generating expectations
of further rises and attracting new buyers . . .' (Eatwell *et al.*, 1987 vol. 1,
p. 281). Another definition is that a bubble exists 'if the reason that the
price is high today is *only* because investors believe that the selling price
will be high tomorrow – when fundamental factors do not . . . justify such
a price' (Stiglitz, 1990, p. 13).

The examples of bubbles which are often quoted are the South Sea
Bubble in London in the 1720s and tulipomania in seventeenth-century
Holland (for a description of some other historical bubbles, see Garber,
1990). In seventeenth-century Holland tulips became very fashionable
and rare strains were bought and sold for breeding. Prices inflated and
tulips became assets; the expectation of rising prices led to increased
demand and thus to a self-fulfilling price rise – which for a time appeared
to be inexorable. Eventually prices became huge and the bubble burst –
prices started falling and led to an expectation of falling prices – leading
to self-fulfilling price falls as traders sought to sell at any price.

---

the EMH has been overstated. Blanchard and Watson (1982, p. 295)
claim that 'Rationality both of behaviour and also of expectations often
does not imply that the price of an asset be equal to its fundamental
value. In other words, there can be rational deviations from this value.'
These 'rational deviations' have been described as rational bubbles.
Much of the literature surrounding bubbles is highly technical; one aim
of this chapter is to summarise the reasons for bubble-like patterns in
asset prices or overshooting suggested in this literature. First, bubbles
are defined in box 3. In this book the term bubble is used to describe a
steep and persistent increase in the price of an asset which is followed
by a sharp fall, whatever the causes of the price movements.

Rational bubbles

The EMH implies that any potential excess returns will be arbitraged
away. Blanchard and Watson (1982) propose a scenario in which
deviations from fundamental values can occur but without creating
possibilities for arbitrage. Consider a price that is deviating upwards
from its fundamental value; the probability of a loss from a fall in price
increases, and thus the investment at these higher prices becomes more
risky; in order to compensate for this increasing risk, the price must
accelerate upwards. If some agents start to withdraw from the market

as market risk increases then the price will be required to grow even faster to prevent a collapse. Some authors have considered the possibility that deviations away from the fundamental prices can be prompted by irrelevant, random events. Hamilton (1986) considers it rational to select stock on the basis of the Super Bowl result if that is what everyone else is doing, because only by behaving in the same way can one hope to achieve the expected return.[1]

These theories invite the question of why investors knowing the price of the asset exceeds its fundamental value, should expect that other people will continue to buy the asset, that its price will go on rising for a time, *and* that they will be able to *beat the gun* in selling before the price falls.

Behaviour

Bull and bear markets

Theories of rational bubbles beg questions about the existence and effects of irrational behaviour. The terms bull market and bear market, which have connotations of irrational behaviour, in the everyday sense of that term, are used very frequently by commentators on the market. Prices rise, or bubble, during bull markets and fall, or burst, during bear markets. Periods of rising and falling prices can be distinguished in past movements of stock market prices, but the longevity of such bull and bear phases varies and cannot be predicted *accurately* while they are in progress from rules based on statistical analysis of earlier data.[2]

The theories which assume rational behaviour to explain bubbles conflict with Keynes's description of the flavour of bull and bear markets:

> There is a great deal of fear psychology about just now. Prices bear very little relationship to ultimate values or even to reasonable forecasts of ultimate values. They are determined by indefinite anxieties, chance market conditions, and whether some urgent selling comes on the market bare of buyers. Just as many people were quite willing in the boom, not only to value shares on the basis of a single year's earnings but to assume that increases in earnings would continue geometrically, so now they are ready to estimate capital values on today's earnings and to assume the decreases will continue geometrically. (From a memorandum for the Board of National Mutual, 18 February 1931. CW, XII, p. 17)

There are other possible explanations for changes of mood among investors. Some investors could be affected by success and failure: psychologically, it could be easier for an investor to invest additional funds when his existing investments are appreciating than when they are falling in value. Apart from the investments an investor owns he may have a list of other investments he considers attractive: if the price of one of these investments rises the investor could decide to *act* before he loses out on any further gains. When shares are rising an investor could consider he is only risking profits (unrealised capital appreciation): when shares are falling he could consider he is throwing good money after bad (the reason is summed-up in the proverb, 'once bitten, twice shy'). More simply, during what they perceive as a bull market, investors could become greedy and act as risk lovers, while during a bear market they could be fearful and risk averse. These patterns of behaviour would not be unique to stock market investors – many UK and Australian industrialists over-expanded their companies during the 1980s in response to readily available credit and initial successes.

Shocks affect people's reactions and decisions. In practice, investors select the information to use; a sharp fall in the prices of shares could lead shareholders to reconsider the reasons they were holding shares and to decide to sell them. Previously they could have focused on the growth of earnings of companies and ignored the current value of the assets owned by the companies, but the shock could lead them to consider the value of the assets owned by companies in relation to the liabilities and share prices of the companies. People may filter information; when share prices have been rising, unfavourable information is ignored or played down. Or the effect may be simpler: the shock could lead some investors to concentrate on gloomy possibilities and play safe by holding cash rather than investing in shares. Such decisions are irrational in the sense that investors are not consistent; they may not react to identical information about an economy or firms received during a bull and a bear market in the same way. Once the assumption of rationality is abandoned there are many possibilities; some investors could treat certain or all of their investments as gambles; they could prefer an investment which carries the possibility of obtaining large gains to an investment with the prospect of higher average but fixed returns and they may not make realistic assessments of the chances of profits and losses.

Professional investment managers

The extent to which fund managers dominate trading on the stock exchange was described in the Introduction. The rationality and psychology of fund managers is now of great importance for the operation of the market. Fund managers might be expected to be less swayed by irrational influences as their own money is not at risk. In practice, however, their jobs may be in danger if their performance is poor and so they could be subject to similar impulses. If, for whatever reason, their performance begins to deteriorate, they may have little to lose by taking larger risks. Efficient investment houses, will, of course, have procedures in place to prevent such activities. Alternatively, some fund managers could be attracted to their career by the possibility of participating in a form of gambling, entering into transactions involving risk and uncertainty, but this invites the question of whether people can obtain the satisfaction provided by gambling if they gamble on behalf of other agents. One answer is that the pay of fund managers is, in part, usually related to the performance of the investments they select, so they do gain by winning. (The investment practices of investment managers were the subject of a survey the results of which are reported in part III.)

Noise trading

One explanation for share prices overshooting (bubbling) could run along the lines that some investors infer information from changes in share prices and base their expectations for changes in share prices on past changes. For example, some investors may extrapolate recent changes in share prices. Given the statistical evidence that shows it is not possible to predict future movements of prices at all accurately from past movements, predicting price movements from past changes in prices is not a rational investment strategy. This reaction of investors has been encapsulated as 'the trend is your friend' syndrome and been given the name 'noise trading'; although it contrasts with Keynes's claim that agents assume that the existing set of, or structure of, market prices is correct, it is within the spirit of Keynes's analysis. Investors may extrapolate trends for several reasons.

1   past performance is the best guide some investors have; they have no basis for assessing economic and industrial information and for making better assessments;

2   some investors gear their investments; as prices change, the value of their security changes, and they keep their borrowing in line with the value of their security by buying or selling. They are in a position to increase their borrowing when prices rise and may have to sell when prices fall to maintain their cover to satisfy lenders or to protect themselves against a further fall in share prices. This investment strategy may be rational if the investors have reasons to believe that the investments they hold are undervalued in the market and that the true value of the investments will be realised by other investors later. (There is evidence that some of Keynes's investment decisions were influenced in this way; see, for example, CW, XII, pp. 27–9.) An investor who gears up his investments is liable to be caught and forced to sell if he does not foresee a fall in the market;

3   some investors, including some institutional investors, use charts and

computer programmes and such techniques as stop-loss selling (investors set a price below the market price and sell if the market price falls to the price) which implies that at least these investors believe that trends can be extrapolated from past experience. However, some chartists may use other information about the state of the market and the psychology of investors to interpret their charts and not rely only on past patterns of price changes being repeated;

4   as noted above, some investors investing in equities may have a gambling, risk-loving motivation and some of these investors may assess the odds of winning – achieving large gains – from recent movements in share prices.

When changes in stock prices reflect both information and noise traders' demands, arbitrage ceases to be riskless as arbitrageurs cannot equalise returns between substitute portfolios since substitute port-folios do not exist. Black (1986) claims that the further away stocks get from their fundamental values the more aggressive the noise traders become – paradoxically, the rate of return will depend upon the rate of return – if price falls are large and fast, noise traders will perceive them and speed them up; if the falls are small and slow they will be unsure of what they see and will not take large short positions. Also, the persist-ence of trends may influence noise traders: the longer a trend has persisted, the greater may be the confidence of the noise trader in a continuation of the trend.

Other reasons for overshooting

Another possible explanation for overshooting is that the response of households' spending on consumption and firms' expenditure on investment to changes in interest rates is slow, and so interest rates are lowered below their long-term equilibrium to stimulate the economy quickly to meet political objectives. As other asset prices are affected by interest rates, they too may overshoot as investors misjudge the dur-ation of low interest rates.

If fund managers and other informed investors believe that bull and bear markets and overshooting occur, for whatever reason, they may attempt to predict and anticipate swings in market movements. Their actions will affect the timing of the movements and the extent of the swings.

Information

One possible reason why prices of stock market securities may not be efficient in the sense of reflecting the real value of shares, *if that could be calculated*, is that investors do not use all of the information available all of the time. One reason why investors use a limited range of information is that the costs of assimilating and using more information could exceed the benefits.

Grossman and Stiglitz (1980) have described 'a model in which there is an equilibrium degree of disequilibrium'. Since collecting and analysing information is a costly exercise, individuals will only perform this function if the rewards exceed the costs. In their model, 'prices perform a well-articulated role in conveying information from the informed to the uninformed. When informed individuals observe information that the return to a security is going to be high, they bid its price up . . . thus the price system makes publicly available the information obtained by informed individuals to the uninformed'. The uninformed obtain the information without incurring costs and obtain part of the benefits; the informed individuals receive only a part of the benefits of collecting and analysing information and so there will be suboptimal collection and analysis of information.

In practice, it is impossible for most, let alone all, investors to assimilate all of the vast quantity of available information which is relevant to security prices. But, although investors do not use all the information available, the large number of investors all using information drawn from the pool of information available could result in an efficient market; but this is not an inevitable outcome, as some relevant information may not be acted upon.

International linkages

In practice, investors must have regard to the increasing internationalisation of security markets. Increased integration has reflected the removal of controls on the international movement of capital by the UK and other governments. The shares of leading UK companies are now quoted on foreign stock markets and vice versa; more important, movements of UK share prices are influenced to a greater extent by movements of share prices on Wall Street and other overseas markets. One effect of the greater international integration of stock markets is that the information relevant to investment decisions in UK shares has expanded to include information about foreign securities and markets. For traders without the in-depth knowledge required to interpret foreign news it may be necessary to infer foreign information from share price movements and act as noise traders.

Market makers

One explanation for fluctuations in share prices is that market makers have an interest in volatile share prices. If some investors respond to movements in share prices in an apparently perverse way, wishing to buy more when prices rise and sell more when they fall (noise trading), market makers can create business by moving share prices. Some investors may react to changes in share prices in this way for the reasons given above, because they assume that other investors have been buying or selling shares and causing the movements in share prices and that these investors have information about companies to which they do not have access: the changes in share prices provide information for these investors.

Self-justifying changes in share prices

Causation could go the other way; following Keynes, changes in share prices may lead to changes in investment and consumption and so affect fundamentals and the profits of companies: changes in share prices could be self-justifying. Changes in asset prices change wealth and have wealth effects, and they affect the confidence of consumers and businessmen.[3] In fact, the effects of changes in share prices on consumers' expenditure could be more important than the effects on investment which were emphasised by Keynes, at least in the short run.

Changes in the price of the shares of a single company can also be self-justifying. A fall can make suppliers reluctant to deal with the company if they interpret the fall as a response to the company encountering difficulties which could lead to its defaulting on its liabilities. Conversely, a rise in the price of a company's shares can enable or encourage its directors to make a takeover which they could or would not make if the price were lower, and give the company credibility with its customers; this may be important if the company enters into long-term contracts with its customers. Similarly, the confidence and enthusiasm of employees may be increased if the price of a company's shares rises; if the price falls sharply, they may be tempted to consider alternative jobs.

Changes in share prices could be self-justifying, but what causes the changes in prices in the first place? If changes in prices are self-justifying, prices are likely to be unstable, because once a change in prices has taken place the new level of prices will be justified. In practice, of course, changes in share prices are not always or completely self-justifying.

Takeovers

Takeover bids are usually made at a premium to the pre-bid price of the target companies' shares. Changing assessments of the likelihood of a takeover can lead to fluctuations in the price of the shares of individual companies. A spate of takeovers may for a time raise share prices generally, as investors bid up the prices of shares of companies which they expect may be taken over.

The supply of equities

So far in this book the explanation for the volatility of share prices has been in terms of the forces affecting demand for shares from investors. A feature of the stock market is that the total stock of shares is inelastic – the supply of new shares does not respond rapidly to changes in prices. Certainly, new issues of shares are made and directors of firms do tend to raise new capital or float their companies when share prices are high, but the response is not rapid, partly because it takes time to prepare prospectuses, etc. When share prices are considered by the directors of companies to be low, companies may buy in more of their own shares and reduce the supply. Nevertheless, the supply of new shares is very much more inelastic then the supply of, say, new cars to the market, and this inelasticity of supply exacerbates changes in prices caused by changes in demand.

The Press

Large sections of many newspapers are devoted to reporting financial news and views. Newspapers are read by investors and if fund managers and other investors were to act on the same advice in the financial columns this could lead to herd-type behaviour and fluctuations in share prices. The role of the Press in generating fluctuations of share prices could be significant and is considered in chapter 15.

Questions suggested by this chapter to bear in mind are:

1   Do investors always act rationally?
2   Do share price movements provide 'information' for investors and, if so, why?
3   Do share price movements influence investors' decisions to buy or sell shares?
4   How important is the influence of the Press in causing movements in share prices?
5   What role do market makers have in creating movements in share prices?

Part II
Markets and returns on investments

---

4 The volatility of share prices

Stock market performance before and after 1936

Before describing the volatility of share prices, the movements of the prices of UK securities before and after 1936, the year Keynes's *General Theory* was published, are summarised to distinguish the trends around which fluctuations occurred (table 4.1). A feature of the data is the rise in bond prices during the 1919–36 period and the falls during both the post-1936 periods, which is, of course, related to falling consumer prices during the period to 1936 and the subsequent inflation. During the first and third periods prices of equities rose.

The volatility of share prices

The purpose of the analyses reported in this chapter is to quantify the extent of the fluctuations in share prices. First, the movements of broadly-based indices of share prices are considered; these would not be expected to move significantly in response to news which relates to a single company unless the company were regarded as a bell-wether for other companies. (For example, reports of ICI's results and prospects are often seen as providing a guide to the performance and prospects for UK companies generally.)

Table 4.2 records some recent sharp, daily movements of indices for the largest international share markets and table 4.3 summarises changes in share prices between June 1987 and June 1991 to put the daily movements in a longer-term perspective. The magnitude of the crash in 1987 was unusual, but there are many examples of movements of several per cent in a single day. How can such large movements be explained? The comments reported in table 4.2 were culled from

Table 4.1. *Market performance*

	1919–1936	1936–1950	1950–1990
Average annual rate of inflation (consumer prices)	− 1.8	+ 5.2	+ 6.8
Average annual rate of growth of real GDP	+ 1.9[a]	+ 1.9	+ 2.5
Average annual percentage increase in			
nominal equity prices	+ 2.8	+ 0.1	+ 9.4
real equity prices	+ 5.2	− 4.8	+ 2.7
Average annual percentage change in prices of long-term government bonds (capital gain(+) loss(−))	+ 2.7	− 1.3	− 2.8

	1919	1936	1950	1990
Dividend yield on equities		(4.0)[b]	(5.2)[b]	3.4
Interest yield on bonds	4.6	2.9	3.5	9.5
Yield gap		(1.1)[b]	(1.7)[b]	− 6.1

Notes: [a] 1920–36.
[b] The dividend yield was estimated from data for a small sample of companies.
Sources: Appendix A, LCES, 1971 and *Economic Trends*, various issues.

contemporary comments in the *Financial Times*. To take one example, the UK market jumped by 5.5% when UK entry to the ERM was announced, but most of this rise was soon reversed. Plainly, both of these movements cannot reflect changes in the effects on UK companies of ERM membership. Also, UK membership of the ERM was expected, so why was it not incorporated in market prices before the announcement of entry? At a superficial level, at least, such large movements of share prices are not compatible with the EMH. The table shows that large share price movements are not unique to the London Stock Market: they have occurred elsewhere.

A more general indication of the fluctuations in indices of share prices is given in table 4.4 which records the month-to-month movement of nominal share prices. Between the end of 1918 and the end of 1990 the average monthly increase in share prices was 0.4% and yet for only 170 of the 864 months was the change in share prices between − 0.9% and 1%. For 210 observations, 24% of the total, the change was less than − 5% or more than 5.01%. The large movements of share

Table 4.2. *Movements of share prices*

Index and date[a]	Change (%)	Reasons reported in *Financial Times*
USA: Dow Jones Index		
12–15/10/87	− 4.7	The crash
16/10/87	− 4.6	The crash
19/10/87	− 22.6	The crash
20/10/87	+ 5.9 ⎫ 16.6	Large cuts in US interest rates
21/10/87	+ 10.1 ⎭	
26/10/87	− 8.0	Steep falls in share prices abroad
6/8/90	− 3.3	Oil price rise due to Gulf crisis causes inflation fears
16/8/90	− 2.4	Escalation in Gulf crisis
8–11/10/90	− 6.3	Escalation in Gulf crisis
8–12/11/90	+ 4.0	Falls in price of oil
UK: FT–Actuaries 500 Share Index		
19–20/10/87	− 19.7	The crash
21/10/87	+ 6.0	The crash
26/10/87	− 7.0	The crash
19–23/2/90	− 3.8	US treasury report of inflation + weak Japanese share prices
14–18/5/90	+ 4.3	Prospect of ERM entry (Mrs Thatcher drops veto on entry)
6/8/90	− 2.8	Oil price rise due to Gulf crisis
20/9/90	− 2.2	Pohl makes anti-UK ERM entry speech
5–8/10/90	+ 5.5	UK entry into ERM
9–11/10/90	− 4.9	Realignment after euphoria associated with ERM
20–23/11/90	+ 2.4	Mrs Thatcher's resignation
Germany: DAX Index		
19–20/10/87	− 11.0	The crash
21/10/87	+ 6.6	The crash
26/10/87	− 5.8	The crash
19–23/2/90	− 4.3	Problems in bond market due to unification spill over into equities
23/4/90	− 2.5	Doubts on German unity
6/8/90	− 5.4	Oil price rise due to Gulf crisis
21/8/90	− 5.2	Gulf-related rumours and heavy investment selling
25/9/90	− 4.4	Gulf uncertainty and little foreign support in market
9–10/10/90	− 4.0	Uninspiring company news

Table 4.2. (*cont.*)

Japan: Nikkei–Dow		
19–20/10/87	− 16.9	The crash
21/10/87	+ 9.3	The crash
26/10/87	− 4.3	The crash
26/2/90	− 4.5	Weak yen
19–23/3/90	− 6.9	Weak yen, rising short-term interest rates, rumours of large speculators in trouble
2/4/90	− 6.6	Weak yen, worries about interest rate and rumours that insurance companies were selling bank shares
19–20/4/90	+ 5.3	Demand for shipping and steel shares
22–30/7/90	− 6.1	Fears of monetary squeeze, insurance companies move out of bank shares
9/8/90	− 3.1	Gulf-related oil price rises
13/8/90	− 4.2	Gulf-related oil price rises
15/8/90	+ 5.4	Gulf-related oil price falls
23/8/90	− 5.8	Gulf-related oil price rises
2/10/90	+ 13.2	Finance minister announces measures to support markets, price of oil falls and Wall Street rises
15–19/10/90	+ 5.9	Optimism over Gulf-oil price fall
22–23/10/90	+ 3.3	Optimism over Gulf-oil price fall
6–8/11/90	− 4.2	Pessimism over Gulf situation
13/11/90	+ 4.5	Strong yen, firm bond prices, lower oil price and rise on Wall Street the previous day

Note: The dates are given in accordance with UK usage, with the month preceded by the day and followed by the year.

prices relative to the average change also applies during the 1980s. On nine occasions, 7% of the observations, share prices fell by more than 5% compared to the average increase per month of 1.1%. Again, the magnitude of the movements of share prices seems excessive in the sense that rational response to new information would not justify the movements which over time were largely self-cancelling.

Changes in the volatility of share prices

The volatility of share prices could change for a number of reasons. For example, a change in the proportion of investment funds managed by professional fund managers rather than by private investors could,

Table 4.3. *Changes in share prices, 1987–1991*

Index	1987 1 June	1987 1 Oct.	1987 31 Dec.	1989 31 Dec.	1990 30 Dec.	1991 30 June
USA						
Standard & Poor's	242.17	327.33	247.08	363.16	330.22	371.00
		(35.2)	(2.0)	(50.0)	(36.4)	(53.3)
UK						
FT–Actuaries	915.61	1,330.66	957.66	1,277.03	1,137.75	1,302.18
All Share		(45.3)	(4.6)	(39.5)	(24.3)	(42.2)
Germany						
DAX	678.57	645.86	425.18	782.21	603.06	682.47
		(−4.8)	(−37.3)	(15.3)	(−11.1)	(0.6)
Japan						
Nikkei–Dow	18,820.65	25,721.74	21,564.0	32,891.12	23,848.71	23,290.96
		(36.7)	(14.6)	(74.8)	(26.7)	(23.8)

Note: The figures in brackets are percentage changes from 1 June 1987

for reasons outlined earlier in the book, affect volatility. If the volatility of the profitability of companies increases, that could lead to greater volatility of share prices and greater instability of monetary conditions, and/or exchange rates could have a similar impact.

The simple comparisons of month-to-month percentage changes in share prices in table 4.4 is too crude to indicate whether there has been an increase or reduction in volatility, but they do suggest that there was not a substantial increase or reduction in large movements during the latest period 1980 to 1990.[1] A recent study for OECD countries concluded that during the period 1961 to 1989 'the highest average monthly volatility was recorded in the post-1985 period for 11 of the 15 countries included', but that 'the elevated average [was] caused by transitory increases in volatility' (Kupiec, 1991). The increase in the proportion of investments controlled by professional fund managers does not seem to have damped down the volatility of share prices but any change attributable to more funds being managed by institutions could be offset by other changes which affect the volatility of share prices.

Shiller's test of the efficiency of markets

Whether or not movements of share prices are excessive cannot be proved in the abstract: the actual movements of prices have to be related to the expected movements, given a theory of the determination

Table 4.4. *Month-to-month percentage changes in share prices*

Percentage change in share prices	Dec.1918 to Dec. 1990	Dec. 1918 to Dec. 1936	(Dec. 1918 to Dec. 1923)	Dec. 1936 to Dec. 1960	Dec. 1960 to Dec. 1970	Dec. 1970 to Dec. 1980	Dec. 1980 to Dec. 1990
less than −20	3	0	(0)	1	1	0	1
−19.9 to −10	16	3	(2)	5	3	5	0
−9.9 to −5	72	16	(4)	21	11	16	8
−4.9 to −1	205	55	(14)	65	25	31	29
−0.9 to 0	78	27	(11)	24	14	7	6
0.01 to 1	92	30	(8)	30	12	9	11
1.01 to 5	279	62	(12)	109	38	28	42
5.01 to 10	99	18	(6)	28	16	16	21
10.01 to 20	18	5	(3)	4	0	7	2
20.01 to 30	1	0	(0)	1	0	0	
30.01 to 40	0	0	(0)	0	0	0	0
40.01 to 50	1	0	(0)	0	0	1	0
Total number of periods	864	216	(60)	288	120	120	120
Average month-to-month percentage change in share prices	+0.4	+0.2	+0.1	+0.4	+0.4	+0.3	+1.1

Note: The date from which the percentage changes are calculated are average prices for working days during each month for the period since July 1970. Earlier data are based on end-of-month prices.

Sources: BZW, 1988; *Economic Trends*, various issues.

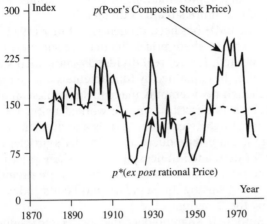

Figure 4.1 Detrended indices of US share prices and dividends (1). Real Standard and Poor's Composite Stock Price Index and *ex post* rational price, 1871–1979, both detrended by dividing a long-run exponential growth factor. The variable p^* is the present value of actual subsequent real detrended dividends, subject to an assumption about the present value in 1979 of dividends thereafter. Source: Shiller, 1981.

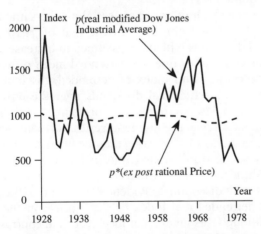

Figure 4.2 Detrended indices of US share prices and dividends (2). Real modified Dow Jones Industrial Average and *ex post* rational price, 1928–79, both detrended by dividing a long-run exponential growth factor. The variable p^* is the present value of actual subsequent real detrended dividends, subject to an assumption about the present value in 1979 of dividends thereafter. Source: Shiller, 1981.

of share prices. As a first approximation, share prices should reflect the discounted value of the future stream of dividends.

Shiller's test of the EMH has been influential. Shiller (1981, p. 241) argued that, since real US share prices fluctuate about their trend far more than do discounted, future, real dividends, movements of share prices cannot therefore be explained by fundamentals and in that sense are excessive. Although no attempt is made to summarise all the tests of the EMH, Shiller's is described and re-worked using UK data to illustrate the relationship between share prices and dividends.

Figures 4.1 and 4.2 are reproduced from Shiller's article; the continuous lines are for detrended indices of US real share prices and the broken lines for detrended indices of discounted future dividends for the periods 1870 to 1978 using the Standard and Poor's Index, and for 1928 to 1978 using the Dow Jones Index.

According to Shiller, if shareholders had perfect foresight, share prices would move closely in line with the discounted stream of future dividends. In reality, investors do not have perfect foresight about future dividends, but the extent to which prices fluctuate more than discounted dividends which show a stable growth path is startling. Shiller's article seems to be an original and simple way of demonstrating that there are excessive fluctuations in share prices, market failure and failure of the EMH.

Figure 4.3 shows the result of two exercises along the same lines as Shiller's based on UK data from 1926 to the end of 1990 and an extrapolation of real dividends which are assumed to increase at 4.0% p.a. from 1990. The continuous line is a detrended index of real share prices and the broken line is an index of detrended, discounted real dividends. For each year actual real dividends over the ensuing 21 years were discounted at 3% p.a. to give the discounted real dividend series. As in Shiller's exercise, the dividend series fluctuates less than the index of share prices, again suggesting that the fluctuations in share prices are excessive. The third, dotted line in figure 4.3 is a closer approximation to Shiller's exercise which set 'an arbitrary value for the terminal value' of future discounted dividends at the end of the period. Here the expected detrended real index of share prices at the end of 1990 was used. Although this gives a damped cycle and contrasts with the movement of detrended real share prices, the significance of the comparison is questionable, because a large part of the valuation of detrended, discounted real dividends turns on the value of the shares at the end of the period. The proportion rises from 20% in 1926 to 43% in 1960 and 96% in 1990.

Let us consider the raw, nominal data: figure 4.4 shows the index of nominal share prices and the index of actual dividends. Inflation in the UK has been faster than in the US and therefore has had a greater

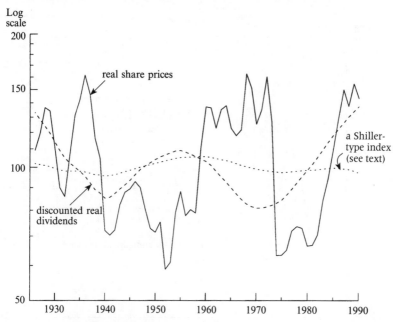

Figure 4.3 Detrended indices of real share prices and discounted real dividends.

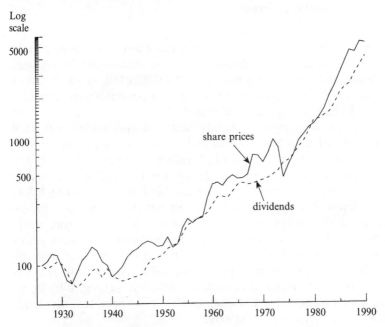

Figure 4.4 Indices of nominal share prices and dividends (1926 = 100).

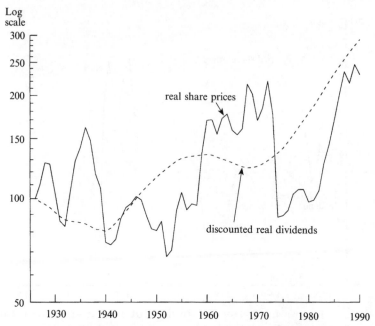

Figure 4.5 Indices of real share prices and discounted real dividends (1926 = 100).

impact on share prices. Here, share prices track dividends quite closely because both increase with inflation, but there are notable divergences between the two series; in particular, the sharp fall in share prices during the early 1970s was not matched by a contemporary or future decline in dividends. Figure 4.5 shows the two series in real terms, but without the trends removed. Plainly, there are protracted and wide deviations of real share prices about their trend. Another feature of this graph is the slow long-term growth of real share prices and discounted real dividends. Real share prices in 1980 were at a similar level to that at the start of the period in 1926. The market failure looks much less severe in figure 4.4 than in figure 4.3 in which a great deal of the movement of the indices has been removed. In the long run, share prices have kept pace with inflation, but the real growth of share prices has been very slow and so, perhaps, it is not surprising that the relationship between real share prices and real discounted dividends is not close. The more interesting question which is suggested by figure 4.5 and which is the subject of chapter 5 is: Why have real dividends and share prices increased so slowly?

Figure 4.6 shows an alternative projection of real dividends. Path A shows the growth of discounted real dividends with real dividends

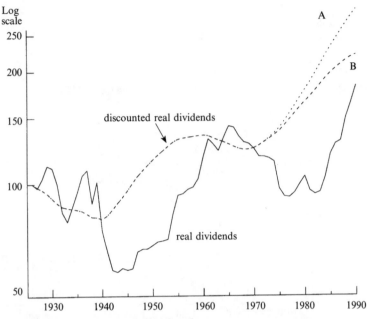

Figure 4.6 Indices of dividends.

increasing at 4.0% p.a. from 1990, and path B with growth of 1.0%
p.a.; 1.0% is the average rate of growth of dividends between 1926 and
1990. The significant point is that the broad conclusions of the exercise
are not affected by the assumption about the future rate of growth of
real dividends. (Between 1926 and 1980, the long-term rate of growth
of dividends was low for reasons which are described in chapter 5 and
which may not be repeated during the next 20 years, while the growth
of dividends during the 1980s was exceptionally rapid.)

The real discount rate

A single discount rate of 3% was used for the exercise illustrated in
figure 4.3. Shiller considered whether plausible changes in the real
discount rate through time could explain the divergence between
detrended, real share prices and detrended, real dividends and concluded that they could not. Since 1981 many econometric tests have
been used to test the relationship between share prices and dividends.
No attempt is made here to summarise this rapidly developing literature.[2] Instead, the relationship between share prices and the money
supply is examined; these analyses are inconclusive and some readers
may wish to pass over the next section.

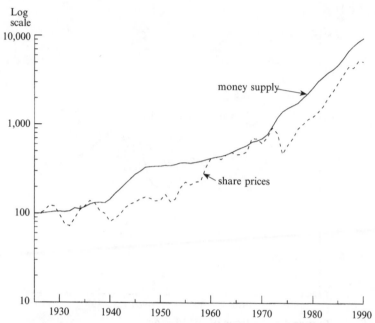

**Figure 4.7 Indices of the money supply, M3, and share prices
(1926 = 100).**

The money supply

Figures 4.7 to 4.10 plot series of the money supply, share prices and
dividends. Figure 4.7 shows the growth of the money supply and share
prices in nominal terms. As would be expected, the movements of the
two series have been similar over the period as a whole but there are
some marked divergences. Figure 4.8, showing the year-to-year percentage changes in the two series, provides a test of any causal link –
whether increases in the money supply lead to increases in share
prices. Generally, the movements of share prices are sharper than those
for the money supply; the two series are positively related but the
relationship is not close. (Where Y_t is the percentage change in share
prices between year 0 and year 1 and X_t is the percentage change in the
money supply between the same years, $Y_t = 3.78 + 0.508X_t (R^2 = 0.04)$.)
One explanation for the lack of a relationship is that the extent to which
changes in the money supply are anticipated or unexpected varies at
different times and affects the timing of any effects.

Figures 4.9 and 4.10 look at the relationship between the real money
supply and dividends. An increase in the real money supply could lead
to an increase in share prices by increasing economic activity, profits

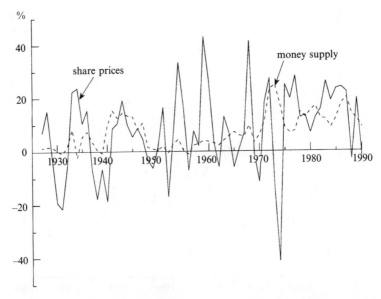

Figure 4.8 Year-to-year percentage changes in share prices and the money supply, M3.

and dividends and/or by increasing share (and other asset) prices relative to income from those assets. Here the second relationship is considered. Figure 4.9 shows that during the two episodes of most rapid growth of the real money supply (circa 1943 and the 1980s) yields did fall, but otherwise the two series are not closely related. Nor do changes in the real money supply explain the divergences between real share prices and discounted real dividends in figure 4.10.

The results of the simple tests in this section to explain fluctuations in real share prices in terms of changes in the real money supply suggest that the relationships are not straight-forward. Alternatively, the effects are camouflaged by changes in other causal factors or relationships.

Smaller companies

So far broad-based indices of share prices have been considered. Two examples of important sub-sectors of the market will now be examined. It has been shown that there are significant deviations in the movement of the indices of share prices of smaller companies relative to the main share indices such as the FT–Actuaries All Share Index. The weighting system used for the FT–Actuaries All Share Index is based on the

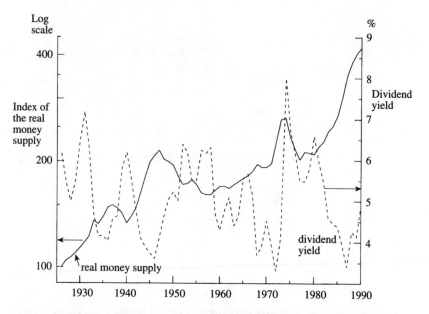

Figure 4.9 Dividend yields and an index of the real money supply.

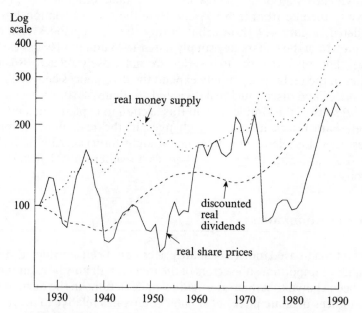

Figure 4.10 Indices of real dividends, real share prices and the real money supply.

market capitalisation of companies so the performance of the shares of large companies dominates this index. (The other market indices also reflect the performance of the shares of large companies. The FT Ordinary Share Index is a geometric average index of the shares of 30 leading companies and the FT–SE 100 Index is an arithmetic average index for the 100 largest companies measured by market capitalisation.) The brokers Hoare Govett have prepared an index for smaller companies; over the period 1955 to 1990 their Small Companies' Index outperformed the FT–Actuaries All Share Index by 4.6% per year *compound*. In 27 of the 36 years the return shown by the Small Companies' Index exceeded that on the FT–Actuaries All Share Index. The *differences* in performance were at times large – in 7 out of 35 years the difference exceeded 20%. Plainly, these differences can cause differences in the performance of unit trusts – those which include small companies are likely to do relatively well when small companies do well.

The differences in performance suggest the question: Why have the returns on investments in the shares of small companies exceeded, and varied from, those for large companies? The pattern of annual returns could diverge for several reasons affecting fundamentals. The industrial composition of the two groups of companies differs – the small companies are concentrated in the capital goods sector and have less exposure to consumer products, and markets for capital goods are more cyclical than those for consumer products. Small companies on average have fewer of their assets overseas and rely on bank borrowing for a higher proportion of their capital, so they are hit harder by high UK interest rates. An investment in the shares of individual small companies may be more risky than in those of large companies, so a higher return may be demanded. Finally, there could be fashions in shares: at times when small companies are fashionable the prices of the shares of small companies will rise relative to market indices.

Oil companies

The market can be sub-divided according to the industrial specialisation of companies. An important industrial sub-sector of the market is that for oil companies; during the 1980s the average weight for oil companies in the FT–Actuaries All Share Index was 12%. During and following oil shocks the prices of the shares of oil companies are likely to move differently from those of companies in other sectors – in brief, companies with access to secure oil supplies gain from an oil shock and lose when the relative price of oil falls.

Table 4.5. *How shares moved during 1990*

	Price on 31 Dec. 1990	% change on year	1990 high	1990 low		Price on 31 Dec. 1990	% change on year	1990 high	1990 low
Indices					*(companies continued)*				
FT Ord Index	1673.7	−12.7	1968	1510	Glaxo	848	+8.0	882	669
FT–SE 100	2143.5	−11.5	2463	1990	Grand Met	675	+7.5	681	514
Companies					Guinness	761	+10.9	824	626
ASDA	119	+3.0	137	87	Hanson	185	−18.0	249	177
Allied-Lyons	481	+1.3	520	408	Hawker Siddeley	439	−37.4	741	375
BICC	331	−30.3	488	302	ICI	866	−23.6	1263	805
BOC	485	−13.2	611	438	Lucas Inds	146	−9.5*	174	102
BTR	321	−30.4*	469	263	Marks & Spencer	223	+11.2	272	181
Blue Circle Inds	219	−14.8	271	163	NatWest Bank	267	−23.0	368	227
Boots	320	+17.2	348	247	P & O	536	−15.1	667	462
British Airways	143	−37.3	240	126	Royal Insurance	393	−32.1	588	337
British Gas	225	−5.1	245	185	Smith Beecham A	633	+3.9	634	460
BP	334	−1.2	384	302	Tate & Lyle	274	−4.5	320	233
British Telecom	284	−8.1	316	243	Thorn EMI	677	−12.9	824	570
Cadbury Schweppes	319	−7.8	378	296	Trusthouse Forte	245	−21.2	318	210
Courtaulds	326	+1.6*	391	267					
GKN	329	−25.4	464	285					
GEC	170	−24.8	245	169					

Note: The table shows the percentage movement in the FT 30 Share Index and its constituents during 1990. The FT–SE 100 Index is also shown. Those adjusted for capital change are marked with an asterisk.
Source: Financial Times, January 1991.

Companies

Sectors of the market are made up of individual companies. Marked changes in the relative prices of sectors of the market and of shares of individual companies occur. Table 4.5 illustrates the dispersion of price changes for the shares included in the FT Index; the Index fell by 13% during 1990, a year in which the UK and US economies moved into recession and in which the Iraq Gulf crisis developed. The range of price changes from the beginning to the end of 1990 for the companies which make up the Index was from −37 to +17%. One indicator of the extent of movements is half the range of prices during the year as a percentage of the mid-point of the range. For ASDA, the first company listed in table 4.5, that is 22%.[3]

Table 4.6 summarises the values of this statistic for the FT–Actuaries 500 Share Index companies. (The total number of companies included is 476 because some companies, which were privatised during 1990 and included in the 500 Index at the end of 1990, were not quoted throughout the year.) The median percentage is 24, the average price range is about a quarter either side of the mid-point of the range. Table 4.7 summarises another measure of price variation for the same companies, the percentage change in price between the beginning and end of 1990. (For the FT 30 companies this statistic is shown in the second column of table 4.5 and was 3.0% for ASDA.) The median fall was about 16% for the 500 Index companies but prices for 42 companies (9% of the 476 companies for which the calculation was made) fell by more than a half.

Past fluctuations through time in the returns on a company's shares can be sub-divided between two components – those which can be explained by movements of the markets as a whole and residual fluctuations. The fluctuations which can be explained by the movements of the market are termed the *undiversifiable* risk and are measured by 'beta' and the residual fluctuations are termed the *diversifiable* risk. In brief, estimates of beta for a company's shares are based on regression analysis of *past* prices of the shares and a broadly-based index of share prices for the same period. Beta measures the elasticity of the price of a share relative to changes in the index – a beta of 2 implies that on average the share has increased or fallen by 2% for each change of ±1% in the index. The diversifiable risk is measured by the proportion of the variance of the prices of a company's shares not explained by changes in the market index. It reflects events affecting expectations for returns on the shares of individual companies but not the market as a whole. The important point is that *if* betas based on *past* data do predict *future* movements of the price of a company's shares relative to

Table 4.6. *Frequency distribution of the range of share-price movements during 1990*[a]

Half the range as a percentage of the mid-point of the range	Number of companies
0–9.9	10
10–19.9	142
20–29.9	184
30–39.9	77
40–49.9	37
50–59.9	19
60–99.9	7
Total	476

Note: [a] For the companies in the FT–Actuaries 500 Share Index which were quoted throughout the year.

Table 4.7. *Frequency distribution of the price changes from the start to the end of 1990*[a]

Magnitude of price change	Number of companies
−75.1 to −100	9
−50.1 to −75	33
−25.1 to −50	130
−0.1 to −25	185
0 to 24.9	105
25 to 49.9	13
50 to 99.9	1
Total	476

Note: [a] See table 4.6, note a.

the market, they enable an investor to limit the risks he or she faces because the remaining (specific) risk *can* be avoided by holding a diversified portfolio. Shares of a company with a high beta (average beta is 1) are therefore rated a high-risk investment. If an investor selects shares which have low betas he can expect his shares to fall less than average if the market falls and in this sense the portfolio avoids risk, but if the market rises the portfolio is likely to underperform the market.

The difference in the returns on shares of smaller companies and

Table 4.8. *Betas and the size of companies*[a]

Market capitalisation (£m)	Betas						
	<0.5	0.5–0.75	0.76–0.9	0.91–1.00	1.01–1.10	1.11–1.25	1.26–1.50
11–25	0	1	3	2	4	6	4
26–50	4	10	13	17	14	12	4
51–100	4	18	28	23	21	15	7
101–500	4	17	20	34	40	32	15
501–1,000	0	1	4	3	16	13	5
1,001–10,000	0	4	17	12	13	12	5
10,000+	0	0	3	0	0	1	0
Sum of first three rows		81			81		48
Middle row		41			74		47
Sum of last three rows		29			44		36

Note: [a] For the companies which are included in the FT–Actuaries 500 Index, but excluding companies in the water industry.
Source: Risk Measurement Service, January–March 1991.

shares which make up the market indices has been noted. Tables 4.8 and 4.9 relate beta and a measure of diversifiable risk to the size of companies. Table 4.8 suggests that beta is not greatly affected by size of companies, but the summary figures at the foot of the table do indicate that the shares of smaller companies tend to have lower than average betas. However, this may not mean that they are less risky than the shares of larger companies. The low beta could reflect fewer movements of the prices of smaller companies' shares because they are traded less often and because the spread between the prices at which market makers will buy and sell (the jobbers' turn) is wider for smaller companies. Also, there could be an important distinction between the extent to which the prices of groups of shares respond to large and to small movements in general market prices which is not reflected in the betas.

Table 4.9 indicates that specific risk is negatively but weakly related to size. Shares of companies with high specific risk are concentrated among the smaller companies. In theory, this risk can be avoided by diversification, so it should not reduce the prices of shares in small companies relative to market averages. Note, however, that the data used to make the estimates of riskiness reported in tables 4.8 and 4.9

Table 4.9. *Specific risk and the size of companies*[a]

	Measure of specific risk					
	0–20	21–30	31–40	41–50	51–60	61–90
Market capitalisation (£m)						
11–25	0	3	5	6	3	3
26–50	2	24	32	11	4	1
51–100	18	59	22	11	3	3
101–500	25	82	43	6	6	0
501–1,000	21	20	0	1	0	0
1,001–10,000	38	19	3	3	0	0
10,000+	4	0	0	0	0	0

Note: [a] For the companies which are included in the FT–Actuaries 500 Index, but excluding companies in the water industry.
Source: Risk Measurement Service, January–March 1991.

were monthly returns for the preceding five years to the end of 1990. Until late in this period the economy had not been in the severe recession which would provide a harsh test of risk for many companies in 1991 and 1992.

Tables 4.10 and 4.11 are designed to assess the predictive power of betas and estimates of specific risk. The tables show the relationships between betas and estimates of specific risk based on data for the five years to 31 December, 1989 and movements in share prices during 1990 when the FT–Actuaries All Share Index fell by 14%. Do the historic betas and estimates of specific risk predict which shares will perform relatively badly when share prices fall? The tables suggest very weak negative relationships with some link between high betas and high specific risk and large falls, but further analysis would be required to assess the relationships fully.

In 1990 companies in the aerospace engineering and food retailing sectors had low average betas, 0.78 and 0.80 respectively, while the cyclical motor industry (which includes motor distribution) and the textile industry had high average betas, 1.18 and 1.20.[4] However, if the Efficient Markets Hypothesis applied, cyclical stocks would not be expected to fluctuate *much* more than the other shares because the cycles would be anticipated.

Table 4.10. *The predictive power of betas*[a]

| Betas[b] | Percentage change in price between 31 December 1989 and 31 December 1990 | | | | | | | | |
	−100 to −80.1	−80 to −60.1	−60 to −40.1	−40 to −20.1	−20 to −0.1	0 to 19.9	20 to 39.9	40 to 59.9	Total
				number of companies[c]					
0–0.50	0	3 (1)	1 (3)	2 (5)	12 (6)	2 (3)	0	0	20
0.51–0.75	2 (2)	1 (4)	8 (11)	18 (17)	24 (22)	16 (11)	1 (2)	0	70
0.751–0.90	2 (2)	7 (6)	16 (19)	20 (28)	35 (37)	28 (18)	6 (2)	0	114
0.901–1.00	3 (2)	2 (5)	21 (15)	24 (22)	22 (29)	17 (15)	0 (2)	1	90
1.001–1.10	1 (3)	8 (7)	15 (22)	38 (32)	53 (42)	10 (21)	4 (3)	1	130
1.101–1.25	4 (2)	9 (5)	19 (17)	26 (25)	26 (33)	16 (16)	2 (2)	0	102
1.251–1.50	1 (1)	2 (3)	18 (11)	18 (16)	17 (20)	7 (10)	0 (1)	0	63
1.501 and over	0	0	2 (1)	2 (1)	2 (2)	0 (1)	0	0	6
Total	13	32	100	148	191	96	13	2	595

Notes: [a] The companies included in the analysis are those included in the FT–Actuaries All Share Index but excluding investment trusts. Approximately 30 companies were excluded from the analysis because price data for 1990 could not be traced.
[b] The betas are based on data for 31 December 1984 to 31 December 1989.
[c] The figures in brackets are the expected number of companies in each cell if there was no relationship between betas and the percentage changes in prices during 1990.
Source: Risk Measurement Service, January–March 1990 and January–March 1991.

Table 4.11. *Predictive power of estimates of specific risk*[a]

Specific risk[b]	Percentage change in price between 31 December 1989 and 31 December 1990								
	−100 to −80.1	−80 to −60.1	−60 to −40.1	−40 to −20.1	−20 to 0.1	0 to 19.9	20 to 39.9	40 to 59.9	Total
	number of companies[c]								
0–15	0	2 (1)	1 (2)	3 (3)	6 (4)	2 (2)	0	0	14
16–20	0 (3)	4 (7)	6 (21)	33 (31)	49 (39)	31 (20)	0 (3)	0	123
21–25	0 (3)	8 (8)	19 (26)	45 (38)	60 (49)	20 (25)	1 (3)	0	153
26–30	4 (3)	3 (6)	23 (19)	30 (29)	35 (37)	19 (19)	1 (3)	1	116
31–35	4 (2)	5 (4)	22 (14)	14 (21)	17 (27)	14 (13)	7 (2)	0	83
36–40	0 (1)	4 (3)	12 (8)	10 (12)	14 (15)	5 (8)	3 (1)	0	48
41–45	1 (1)	2 (1)	9 (5)	8 (7)	5 (9)	1 (4)	0 (1)	1	27
46–50	2 (0)	1 (1)	2 (2)	2 (3)	2 (4)	2 (2)	0	0	11
51+	2 (0)	3 (1)	6 (3)	3 (5)	3 (6)	2 (3)	1	0	20
Total	13	32	100	148	191	96	13	2	595

Notes: [a] See footnote a to table 4.10.
[b] Based on data for 31 December 1984 to 31 December 1989.
[c] The figures in brackets are the expected number of companies in each cell if there was no relationship between specific risk and changes in the percentage changes in prices during 1990.
Source: Risk Measurement Service, January–March 1990 and January–March 1991.

Conclusions

In this chapter the extent of fluctuations in share prices has been quantified. The extent of the short-term fluctuations in market prices illustrated in tables 4.2 to 4.4 is not readily explicable in terms of changes in fundamentals alone. Also, there are protracted and wide deviations of real share prices from their long-term trend.

Given the volatility of share prices, investors are faced with a dilemma: should they attempt to forecast which investments/shares will give the highest return over, say, a ten-year time span or should they play the market, trying to predict what the market price will be next week or next month? If an investor can achieve a series of good short-run results, this will add up to a good long-term result and he need not worry whether his decisions to buy and sell are compatible with the long-term prospects for the investments. In any case he may argue that it is not possible to assess the long-term prospects for profits and dividends.

5 The slow growth of real dividends

The growth of real dividends

An important point shown in figure 4.6 and again in figure 5.1 is that between 1926 and 1990 real dividends increased by only 83% (0.95% per year compound). The dividend yield of £6.17 on £100 invested in 1926 would have increased in real terms, but only to £11.27 in 1990 in terms of 1926 consumer prices. This seems an incredibly small increase. (The comparisons start from 1926, the first year for which estimates of the dividend yield on shares were made by Moodies.[1]) Figure 5.1 provides a comparison of the growth of real dividends and real share prices and shows that real share prices increased by 131% between 1926 and 1990. Real share prices thus increased significantly more than real dividends. If the movement of share prices diverges from that of dividends, this reflects changes in the yield on equities: the dividend yield on equities was 6.17% in 1926 and 4.89% in 1990.

Investors, including some fund managers with whom the slow growth of real dividends was discussed, expressed surprise that the growth was so slow. One explanation for their surprise that dividend growth had been so slow since 1926 may have been that they were accustomed to the much more rapid growth of the 1980s. Real dividends were increasing rapidly during the 1980s and may have conferred an illusion of long-term steady growth, especially for fund managers recruited since 1980. By 1980 real dividends on a hypothetical investment in the index described in the Appendix and shown in table A1 column 6 in 1926 had increased by only 4.5%; between 1980 and 1990 there was an increase of 74.8%. Another reason for fund managers' surprise could be that they confuse the growth of real dividends with the rate of growth of the value of hypothetical investments *with income reinvested*. Unit trusts feature calculations of this sort in their publicity in part because it is considered the correct basis for comparing returns on investments. (In fact, the method does not

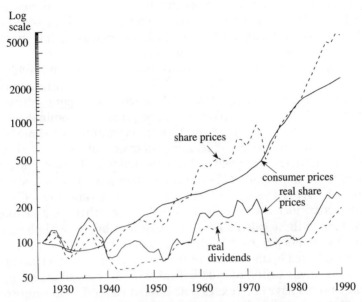

Figure 5.1 Indices of share prices, consumer prices, real share prices and real dividends (1926 = 100).

necessarily reflect the returns on investments obtained by investors who cannot or do not wish to reinvest their income.) Between 1926 and 1990 the index of share prices with *gross* dividends reinvested increased 1295-fold, at a compound rate of 11.8% per annum, and by 57-fold in real terms, at 6.5% per year, compared to the 0.95% growth of real dividends. (Reinvested dividends are assumed to appreciate in line with the index from the time of reinvestment.) These calculations emphasise the positive effects on recorded investment performance of reinvesting (*gross*) dividends. In part, the relative magnitude of the effects of reinvesting dividends reflects the slow growth of real dividends and hence the slow growth of share prices in real terms.

A different implication of the slow growth of real dividends is that in the long run dividends more than kept pace with retail prices – they did not fall in real terms. However, it cannot be assumed that dividends are inflation-proof. Inflation could reduce real profits and dividends if companies were unable fully to pass on increases in their costs in higher prices for the products and services they sell, but in the long run any effects of past inflations to reduce real dividends could have been offset by other forces, including profits earned on ploughed-back profits.

Reverting to the slow growth of real dividends, the figures show that capitalists have had a very small share of the growth of the economy;

the output of the economy as measured by GDP increased by 311% between 1926 and 1990 and real wages per employee rose by 242%. Dividends in aggregate real terms have increased, but most of this increase reflects dividends on new capital issues.

The implication is that profits not distributed as dividends and retained by companies have earned a very low return; equities have been an inflation hedge with only a small real bonus. Through the period 1926 to 1990, ploughed-back profits in nominal terms have averaged out about equal to dividends, as earnings per share have been about twice dividends. If retained profits equal to 5% of share prices had been invested to yield 10% compound in real terms, and dividends had taken a constant 50% of profits, then real dividends should have risen by 5.1% a year and 24-fold between 1926 and 1990, compared to the actual increase of only 83%.[2] However, there is a serious quali-fication to these calculations – the earnings figures and ploughed-back profits are not adjusted for the effects of inflation. In so far as earnings were boosted by the effects of inflation to reduce depreciation charges and by the inclusion of inflation gains on net current assets, ploughed-back profits have been exaggerated: retained profits after adjustment for inflation were less than the nominal ploughed-back profits. It is not possible to assess accurately the extent to which ploughed-back profits were inflation gains, but if it is assumed that a half of ploughed-back profits were, then if companies ploughed back real profits equal to approximately 2.5% of their share prices per year, obtained a 10% compound return on the investment and distributed 75% of profits, real dividends would have increased by 3.1% per year and by 597% over the 64-year period, compared to the actual 83%.

Explanations for the slow growth of real dividends

Earnings and dividends

One explanation for the slow growth of real dividends relates to company earnings: the proportion of earnings paid out as dividends was lower in 1990 than it was in 1926. Real earnings per share rose by about 147% in real terms between 1926 and 1990, compared to the 83% increase in real dividends. The growth of real earnings and real dividends are compared in figure 5.2; although real earnings increased more than real dividends, the increase in real earnings per share averaged only 1.4% per year, again suggesting a poor return on ploughed-back profits. (The faster growth of earnings than dividends may have contributed to the faster growth of share prices than dividends.)

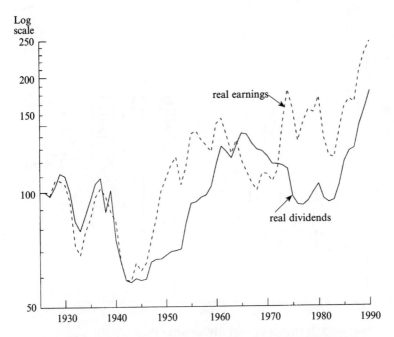

Figure 5.2 Indices of real dividends and real earnings (1926 = 100).

The measurement of profits

In contrast to 1926, in 1990 companies may have been investing a higher proportion of their turnover on R&D, marketing and educating and training their labour force, which will earn profits in the future while reducing current recorded earnings and perhaps dividends. This effect would be muted because similar expenditure in the years before 1990 would give rise to a charge against profits in that year if it had not already been charged against profits.

Takeovers

It is claimed that:

1   the share prices of small companies outperform the share prices of large companies;
2   small companies are more likely to be taken over;
3   acquiring companies pay a premium for acquisitions.

Combining these claims, one explanation could run along the lines that the return on retained earnings of large companies has been squandered by these companies paying over the odds for acquisitions where

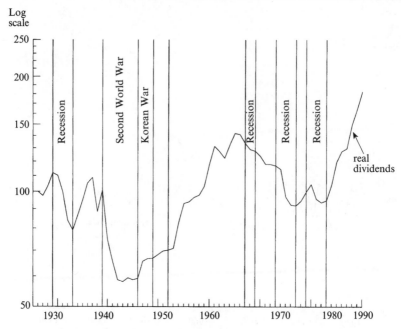

Figure 5.3 Index of real dividends (1926 = 100).

the motivation was to expand the companies rather than add profits. There is a vast literature on the effects of mergers which is inconclusive about their impact, so large effects of this sort are unlikely – though they may well apply to some companies.

Shocks

The explanations given so far do not go far towards solving the mystery of the slow growth of real dividends. An alternative explanation would pinpoint the succession of shocks as the cause of the disappearing retained earnings. The shocks may have destroyed the assets and profits of companies and thus offset some of the growth of earnings attributable to retained earnings. The shocks which are indicated in figures 5.3–5.6 and table 5.1 include the 1930s slump; the Second World War (real dividends fell sharply during the War); socialist policies (real dividends recovered between 1946 and 1951 following the War but did not match the 1939 level until 1959, and they fell during the Labour Governments of the 1960s and 1970s); the oil price shocks (real dividends fell during the recessions following the 1973/4 and 1979/80 oil shocks); and the freeing of world trade.

The two protracted periods of growth of real dividends were 1946–1964 and 1979–1989. During the two long periods of Conservative

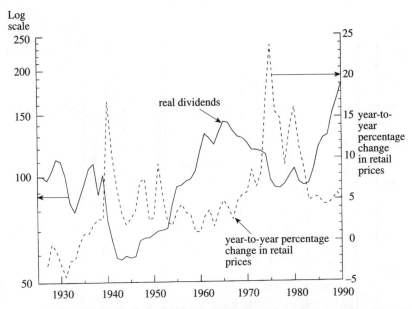

Figure 5.4 Index of real dividends and year-to-year percentage change in retail prices.

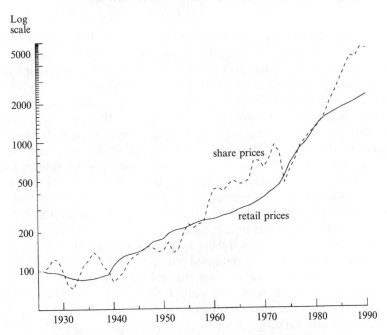

Figure 5.5 Indices of share prices and consumer prices (1926 = 100).

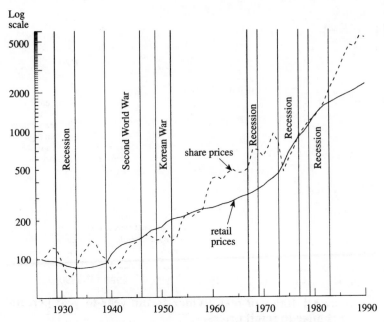

Figure 5.6 Indices of share prices and retail prices.

Governments, 1951–1964 and 1979–1989, both real share prices and real dividends increased. During the 16 post Second World War years with Labour Governments, real dividends fell by 0.3% per year on average and real share prices fell by 0.1% a year. During the 28 years of Conservative Governments real dividends rose at an average annual rate of 4.3% and real share prices at 3.1% a year.[3] Is the explanation for these differences that the periods of Labour Government were more difficult for the economy? A very approximate statistical control of external economic conditions is the US share market – during the 16 years of Labour Governments US real dividends rose by 3.1% a year and during Conservative Governments by 1.8%, according to the Standard and Poor's Index. (In contrast, US share prices fell in real terms by 2.4% a year during periods of Labour Governments in the UK and rose by 5.4% a year in real terms during periods of Conservative Governments.) Reverting to the UK data and leaving aside the period of the Second World War and the recovery in real dividends from 1946 to 1959, real dividends increased by only 1.7% per year between 1959 and 1989. Since 1960 real earnings have fluctuated around a weak upward trend and real dividends which fell between the mid 1960s and the mid 1970s, recovered during the 1980s. (The movements were shown in figure 5.2.)

Table 5.1. *Retail and share prices, dividends and GDP, average annual percentage rates of change*

	1926–30	1930–40	1940–50	1950–60	1960–70	1970–80	1980–89
Consumer prices	−1.8	+1.6	+4.9	+3.5	+4.0	+13.3	+5.9
Share prices	−0.6	−1.8	+5.7	+11.5	+3.9	+7.2	+15.4
Real share prices	+1.2	−3.3	+0.8	+7.7	−0.02	−5.3	+8.9
Real dividends	+2.5	−3.8	−0.9	+5.6	+0.5	−1.7	+5.8
Real GDP	+3.2	+3.8*	−0.2*	+2.7	+3.0	+1.8	+2.4

	1935–40	1940–6	1946–51	1951–64	1964–70	1970–4	1974–9	1979–90
Government	C	N	L	C	L	C	L	C
Consumer prices	+4.9	+4.8	+5.9	+2.9	+4.6	+10.0	+15.3	+6.8
Share prices	−7.6	+10.3	+2.4	+8.8	+3.8	−6.5	+19.7	+14.6
Real share prices	−12.0	+5.2	−3.3	+5.7	−0.7	−15.0	+3.8	+7.3
Real dividends	−4.6	−3.8	+3.3	+5.1	−1.1	−2.0	−2.7	+5.7
Real GDP	+6.4*	−1.0*	+1.5	+3.0	+2.6	+2.5	+2.0	+2.0

	1929–33	1933–9	1939–46	1946–73	1973–7	1979–82	1982–9
	Recession	Recovery	War	Post war boom	1st oil shock	2nd oil shock	Recovery
Consumer prices	−3.0	+1.5	+6.5	+7.0	+17.8	+12.1	+5.7
Share prices	−7.5	+2.0	+5.6	+10.6	+3.0	+11.8	+18.4
Real share prices	−4.8	+0.6	−0.8	+3.4	−12.5	−0.3	+12.9
Real dividends	−8.3	+4.2	−7.4	+4.1	−5.8	−2.1	+8.4
Real GDP	−1.7	+5.3*	+0.9*	+4.1	+0.7	−0.5	+3.6

Note: * Estimates for the years 1939–45 are approximate because they are affected by the Second World War.
Source: Data appendix, and for GDP, *Economic Trends*, Annual Supplement, various issues, LCES, 1971, and Capie and Webber, 1985.

Inflation

The underlying assumption that equities are inflation-proof could be false. During a period of inflation declared profits and earnings exceed real profits and that could explain why the increase in real dividends was so slow in spite of high retained nominal earnings. Earlier in this chapter an adjustment based on a specified assumption was made to nominal profits to allow for the effects of inflation on profits. But this adjustment could underestimate the effects of inflation. During periods of rapid inflation companies may be unable, or fail, to pass on increases in costs, and they may make losses which they are unable to recover

Table 5.2. *Growth of real dividends and inflation, 1960–1990 (percentage changes)*

Country	Period	Dividend yields	Share prices	Consumer prices	Real share prices	Real dividends
UK	1960–70	+5	+47	+47	0	+5
	1970–80	+46	+101	+247	−42	−16
	1980–90	−26	+320	+78	+236	+75
	1960–90	+13	+1141	+808	+95	+54
USA	1960–70	+15	+54	+31	+17	+35
	1970–80	+32	+47	+112	−30	−8
	1980–90	−32	+191	+92	+52	+4
	1960–90	+4	+559	+433	+25	+29
Japan	1960–70	−8	+68	+74	−3	−11
	1970–80	−56	+190	+72	+69	−25
	1980–90	−67	+359	+23	+273	+24
	1960–90	−87	+2137	+268	+508	+19
Germany	1960–70	+120	−4	+29	−26	+64
	1970–80	+32	−6	+64	−43	−25
	1980–90	−35	+206	+29	+137	+54
	1960–90	+89	+176	+173	0	+91
France	1960–70	+45	+4	+49	−30	+1
	1970–80	+20	+45	+151	−42	−31
	1980–90	−35	+469	+84	+209	+101
	1960–90	+13	+758	+588	+25	+40

Sources: For the UK, see Data appendix. For the other countries, *International Financial Statistics*, various issues; *Eurostat; Statistical Yearbook*, 1991 for Japan.

later. During the early 1970s, incomes policies imposed controls on prices, and taxation based on nominal profits could have caused such losses. Real dividends fell sharply during the 1970s simultaneously with faster inflation. Table 5.2 also provides some support for the view that inflation reduces real dividends. Between 1970 and 1980, a period which covers the great world inflation, real dividends fell in all five leading industrial countries. In view of these figures it is little wonder capitalists are hostile to inflation! However, the fall in real dividends was second lowest for the UK, the country with the fastest rate of inflation. Also, the speeding up of inflation during the 1970s was accompanied by recession, and recession rather than inflation could have caused the fall in real dividends. The extent to which recession was the result of faster inflation is difficult to assess.

Competition

A plausible explanation which is difficult to test is that technical progress and competition is continuously destroying sources of profits. At any point in time many firms have some protection from competition – and hence profits – through the control of patents, trade marks, knowledge and factors of production. Other firms seek to break into these markets and in time such positions and profits are eroded.

Components of the Index

So far the movement of the composite FT–Actuaries All Share Index of share prices and the dividend yield for that Index have been considered. The FT–Actuaries All Share Index is sub-divided into 36 sub-sections which show a remarkable diversity of performance. For the period from the formation of the Index in 1962 until December 1990, motors show an increase of 195% in nominal terms while publishing and printing show a 2,859% increase; in real terms, motors fell by 69% as publishing and printing rose by 207%. The performance of motors was, however, dragged down by British Leyland.

It is difficult to distinguish clear patterns: generally, the industrial sectors had a relatively weak performance – general engineering an increase of 270% in nominal terms (and a fall of 62% in real terms), aerospace engineering 299%, metals and metal-forming 312%, and textiles 333%; but electrical engineering showed a nominal rise of 1,820% (a real increase of 99%) and chemicals a rise of 986%. Sectors supplying consumers fared better: brewers and distillers showed an increase of 1,480%, food manufacturers 931%, food retailers 2,163%, health and household 2,460%, and stores 792%.

It is easier to rule out explanations for the differences in performance than to pinpoint explanations for them. They are not attributable to differences in the proportion of profits paid out as dividends or differences in ploughed-back profits per share. Engineering and textiles have faced intense international competition while brewers and food manufacturers sell mainly to the domestic market and face limited competition from imports. This comparison suggests that the shock caused by the freeing of world trade contributed to the slow growth of real dividends and share prices. Pharmaceuticals (which account for the good performance of the health and household sector) and the oil industry include strong UK companies. The good performance of pharmaceuticals and the relatively good performance of chemicals and electrical engineering could have been facilitated by the freeing of world trade, though imports adversely affected parts of these industries.

Conclusions

In this chapter it has been shown that the growth of real dividends and hence share prices was surprisingly slow over the period 1926 to 1990 as a whole. A number of explanations for this result have been listed, but it has not been possible to identify the impact of each of the explanations. The Second World War and oil price shocks seem to have contributed; also, the effects of increased international competition may have eroded profits. The growth of real dividends was more favourable during periods of Conservative Government than during periods of Labour Government.

A reason why the slow long-term growth of real dividends (which did not apply during the 1980s) is important is that it reinforces the priority which fund managers have to give to achieving a satisfactory return on their clients' investments.

6 The undervaluation of equities

A comparison of returns on investments

If it could be shown that the market has persistently undervalued equities relative to other assets, that would be a more serious form of market failure than the excessive volatility of share prices. If equities are undervalued the following consequences ensue:

1   the cost of an important source of capital for companies will be raised. Even assuming that this higher cost is matched by lower interest rates, there are practical constraints on the gearing ratios with which companies operate, and so capital accumulation will be distorted;

2   the choice facing companies, whether to invest internally or externally by takeover, will be artificially weighted towards takeover because the value of acquisitions will be lowered relative to the prices of new assets.

One way to show that equities have in fact been undervalued is to compare the *ex post* return on equities and fixed interest. The method of calculating returns is described in Box 4. In his article, 'On the Structure of the Capital Market' (1962), Farrell used data for the period 1948 to 1961. The period has been extended to 1990 in table 6.1, and a column for building societies has been added, since that is a favourite investment for many investors. The first three columns of the table show nominal and real returns before tax, and the final two columns, in effect, show after income tax returns (but before capital gains tax). There have been short periods (particular, 1972 to 1974) when fixed interest securities have outperformed equities, but during each post-war decade the return on equities has exceeded that for consols and debentures.

During the 1950s the difference in returns was enormous. During the 1960s, 1970s and 1980s the gap between the return on equities and fixed interest securities narrowed and was of the order of 5% per year.

Box 4   Returns on investment

The performance of an investment is measured by the return from the investment which combines both capital gains and the dividends. The gross nominal return on an investment over a period of a year is $((p_{t1} + d_{t1})$ as a percentage of $p_{t0}) - 100$, where p_{t0} is the price of security at the beginning of the year, p_{t1} the price at the end of the year and d_{t1} is the gross dividend received during the year. To calculate the returns on a notional investment in an index, prices are replaced by index numbers and dividends by yields.

The real return on an investment is:
$$\left((100 + \text{ the nominal return}) \times \frac{r_{t0}}{r_{t1}}\right) - 100$$

where r is the retail price or other price index.

The after tax return is calculated by deducting tax at the *standard rate* from the dividend. Similarly, if returns are to be calculated after management charges in the case of managed funds, the annual charges are deducted from the dividend. Usually, returns are reported before capital gains tax because the UK capital gains tax is based on *realised* capital gains and many institutional investors are exempt from the tax, even on realised gains. The return after capital gains tax is calculated by deducting the capital gains tax from the price at the end of the period. The average return for a period of years is calculated as the geometric average of the returns for each of the years: it is the average compound rate of return.

A minor qualification to these estimates of returns is that they are calculated on an annual basis. Dividend and interest income is received during a year and can be reinvested to earn a return until the year end, but this extra income is ignored.

Building societies versus equities

So far, yields for equities and bonds have been compared. Nowadays most private investors do not invest in bonds; their choice is between investment in shares and in building societies. Returns for these investments are shown in the final two columns of table 6.1 and in table 6.2, which compare returns over various periods. For table 6.2, it is assumed that net income is reinvested quarterly – in the case of equities, at current share prices. For equities, net income is after deduction of income tax at the standard rate and for building societies the composite rate is used. (For nearly all of the period the composite rate was in effect net of the standard rate tax for recipients.) Purchases and sales of equities are assumed to be made at the average price for a

Table 6.1. *Security returns*

	Average annual returns (%) before deduction of income tax				
	Consols[a]	Debentures[b]	Equities[c]	Equities after deduction of income tax	Building society deposits
			Nominal[d]		
1951–60	−0.2	0.8	15.6	12.9	3.0
1961–70	1.4	3.1	8.9	6.9	4.1
1971–80	10.0	10.7	14.6	12.4	7.1
1981–90	11.9	13.4	19.3	17.8	8.3
(1972–74)	(−10.8)	(−11.3)	(−24.8)	(−26.4)	(6.1)
			Real[d]		
1951–60	−4.1	−3.1	+11.2	+8.6	−0.9
1961–70	−2.8	−1.2	+4.4	+2.4	−0.2
1971–80	−3.3	−2.7	+0.7	−1.2	−6.0
1981–90	+5.1	+6.6	+12.1	+10.7	+2.1

Notes: [a] 2½% Consols are British Government Stock.
[b] Debentures are 15-year debentures.
[c] Equities are ordinary shares for which the FT–Actuaries 500 Share Index was used.
[d] The figures are for end-December each year.
Source: Financial Times, various issues; *Monthy Digest of Statistics,* various issues.

quarter. Notional transaction costs are charged at 3% on purchases and 2.5% on sales. Recently, transaction costs have been cut by reductions in the rate of stamp duty on transactions, and costs would now be lower for deals much larger than £1,000. The results are representative for an investor with a widespread portfolio of equities or an investment in unit or investment trusts whose performance matches the FT–Actuaries 500 Share Index and with individual transactions averaging about £1,000.

To illustrate the calculations the return on investments for a period of one quarter is described. Table 6.2 shows that the average return on deposits of £1,000 with building societies was £16 a quarter (row 1 column 2); this is the average return for the 120 quarters during the 30-year span. The table also shows that when transaction costs are excluded, the average return on equities was £33; but when transaction

Table 6.2. *Average return[a] on investments of £1,000, 1960–1990 (£s)*

Period	Number of periods averaged[b]	Building society deposits	Equities[c] with no transaction costs		Equities[c] after transaction costs		Equities[c] after transaction costs and capital gains tax at 15%	
1 quarter	120	16	33	(58)	−22	(29)	−17	(28)
1 year	117	66	149	(68)	87	(56)	79	(55)
2 years	113	137	322	(75)	250	(70)	223	(67)
5 years	101	386	1,023	(82)	906	(76)	804	(74)
10 years	81	951	3,039	(95)	2,786	(91)	2,467	(88)
30 years	1	5,872	29,715	(100)	27,283	(100)	24,267	(100)

Notes: [a] Return is the income net of basic rate income tax plus, in the case of equities, capital appreciation.
[b] All the periods available from Q4, 1960 to Q4, 1990.
[c] Figures in brackets are the percentage of periods in which equities win.
Source: author's calculations.

costs are included, the average return on investment in equities for one quarter was negative, −£22. As the period for holding investments lengthens there are fewer periods to include, they overlap and transaction costs are relatively less important. For example, for investments for periods of ten years (row 5), there were 81 observations and the average return on equities was £3,039 before transaction costs, and £2,786 after transaction costs.

The effects of capital gains tax (at 15%) are also illustrated in table 6.2. For this purpose it is assumed that capital gains tax is repaid on losses; in practice, any losses can only be set against realised profits in the same tax year or be carried forward. The rate of capital gains tax and the exemption limit have varied over the period. (Capital gains tax is only paid on realised capital gains in excess of the exemption limit, so it would not be paid by an investor who retained all of his investments.) A hypothetical rate of 15% has been used to provide an indication of the effects of capital gains tax, but many private investors with limited capital avoid paying capital gains tax at least for most of their gains. The effect of capital gains tax is to reduce further the average return on equities and to extend the time it takes for the return on equities to overtake the return on building society deposits.

Table 6.3. *Comparison of nominal returns (after income tax but before capital gains tax or transaction costs)*

| From 31 December | To 31 December | Average annual percentage return | | Periods during which equities win |
		equities with net after tax income reinvested annually	building society deposits with income reinvested	
1960	1963	6.8	3.6	✓
1	4	5.7	3.6	✓
2	5	7.5	3.6	✓
3	6	3.7	3.8	
4	7	5.6	4.0	✓
5	8	18.3	4.2	✓
6	9	12.1	4.5	✓
7	1970	11.2	4.8	✓
8	1	13.6	5.0	✓
9	2	6.2	5.0	✓
1970	3	1.6	5.5	
1	4	− 13.4	6.3	
2	5	0.0	7.2	
3	6	− 2.2	7.2	
4	7	16.8	7.0	✓
5	8	42.1	6.8	✓
6	9	15.1	7.3	✓
7	1980	21.9	8.5	✓
8	1	14.1	9.3	✓
9	2	19.9	9.3	✓
1980	3	24.1	8.0	✓
1	4	24.7	7.7	✓
2	5	26.5	7.8	✓
3	6	24.9	8.2	✓
4	7	20.9	8.1	✓
5	8	15.0	7.5	✓
6	9	18.6	8.0	✓
7	1990	9.2	8.9	✓

Source: author's calculations.

Equities win by a very large margin over the period as a whole. The after capital gains tax return over 30 years was £24,267 for equities, compared to £5,872 for building society deposits (final row columns 2 and 5). They also win for most shorter periods; for example, for

70% of the two-year periods, equities win when the return on equities after capital gains tax is compared to the return from building society deposits.

Table 6.3 gives another comparison of returns on equities and building society deposits; this time investments for a period of three years are compared. The comparisons are for returns after deducting income tax but before capital gains tax and transaction costs. Equities win for 23 of the 28 periods. If the return on equities has to be, say, 2% a year above that for building society deposits to cover transaction costs and the hassle of investing in equities, equities win 20 out of the 28 periods and for 13 of the last 14 periods.

Takeovers

Other evidence that equities have been undervalued is provided by the premia which are paid to the shareholders of acquired companies in takeovers. The fact that acquirers are willing to pay in excess of market prices points to undervaluation, though there are other possible explanations: the increases in efficiency which the acquirers can achieve (Bhagat *et al.*, 1990) or that the motivation of managers making takeovers is to acquire assets and expand their businesses even at the expense of lower profits.

Explanations for an undervaluation of equities

Why do the differences in returns persist? Why do investors repeatedly make the same mistake, or, to use the rational expectations terminology, why do they allow themselves to be fooled repeatedly?

One way to explain the differences in returns is to attribute it to differences in the riskiness of equity and fixed interest investments. For example, Dimson and Marsh (1982) calculate the average annual excess gross return on equities over the yield on Treasury Bills for the period from 1919 to 1979 at 9%, and aver that this is the 'average risk premium'. One interpretation of this claim is that the investors have foreseen the returns of different investments and their volatility and that the higher return on equities reflects the greater risks associated with holding equities – that a holder of equities if forced to sell at a time when equity prices are below trend, such as December 1974, will obtain a lower return than if he or she had invested in Treasury Bills: the relative certainty of the return on Treasury Bills compensates for the lower return.

A second explanation is that the markets for equities and bonds are segmented. Most people wish to keep some part of their wealth in cash or a readily realisable asset and some of the public never consider investing in equities or have too few assets to make it worthwhile. For a variety of reasons, including legal restraints on the selection of investments, prudential and conventional rules adopted by insurance companies or imposed on them by actuaries, institutions' freedom to switch holdings of assets is restricted. (Also, investors hold fixed interest securities or deposits to provide liquidity, or to cover known liabilities, including liabilities expressed in money such as non-profit life assurance contracts. These and other restrictions are described in part III.) Such conventions and restrictions would not determine returns if other investors compensated, if necessary, by selling some securities short. In practice, selling fixed interest securities short and buying equities during most of the period 1919 to 1979 was impracticable or expensive in terms of transaction costs for most investors.

A third explanation is that investors simply failed to foresee the differences in returns in spite of their persistence. Investors could have *over*-assessed the future returns on fixed interest securities and deposits which in the event were often negative because they under-predicted the rate of inflation. In the long run the increase in share prices and retail prices have been similar (see figure 5.1). It is tempting therefore to account for a part of the failure of investors to foresee the relative performance of equities in terms of their under-prediction of the rate of inflation, which could be explained by investors believing repeated government claims that they would control inflation.

All three explanations probably contribute to the differences in returns, but it is not possible to separate their effects. Moreover, if it is true that all three explanations contribute, then estimates of the risk premium based on comparisons of returns on investments are unreliable. If investors underestimated the future returns on equities that would exaggerate the risk premium as estimated from an *ex post* comparison of returns. Also, if the volatility of prices of equities is excessive in relation to changes in fundamentals, as suggested in chapter 4, the risk premium will be inflated.

Conclusion

In retrospect it can be seen that throughout most of the post Second World War period equities have been undervalued relative to other assets, in the sense that in the event returns on equities were far higher than returns on bonds and deposits. The result is difficult to reconcile with the EMH and is consistent with the impossibility of making accurate predictions of future returns on securities. If such undervaluation of the market can persist, persistent undervaluation of individual shares relative to the equity market as a whole may also occur.

An implication of the comparisons of returns reported in this chapter is to reinforce the effects of the slow growth of real dividends reported in the previous chapter. Real dividends have risen slowly during the period 1926 to 1990 as a whole; nevertheless, the return on equities has been higher than those on deposits and gilts for much of the period, so the difficulty of achieving a satisfactory return on investors' funds was intensified.

7 The property market

Introduction

This chapter outlining characteristics of the UK commercial property market has been included to provide a benchmark against which the stock market can be compared. Commercial property includes offices, shops, industrial premises (factories and warehouses) and agricultural property. London dominates the UK office market – it has by far the largest concentration of offices in the UK, while rents for office space in the City and central London are higher than for offices elsewhere. Many premises are owned by the firms which use them in the course of their trade; other owners include property companies – companies which specialise in the development, ownership and leasing of property – and pension funds and insurance companies that hold properties which they lease as investments. Although international property investment has increased, it is on a smaller scale than the globalisation of the bond and equity markets.

The commercial property market is much less liquid than the stock market, the size of transactions is larger and transaction costs are higher. Even when the market for property is buoyant it may take two or three months to arrange the sale of a property and, when the property market is in recession, it may take much longer. The rate of stamp duty on sales of property is 1% and total transaction costs for the seller and buyer together are estimated to be about 6%. By international standards, though, UK transaction costs for property deals are moderate and in some European countries they are substantially higher. In the case of shares, a major component of transaction costs is 'the jobbers' turn' (the difference between the buying and selling prices at which market makers deal); in contrast, most property deals are negotiated by agents between principals and so there is no equivalent of the jobbers' turn. Another contrast is that shares in a company are uniform: all the ordinary shares in ICI carry the same rights, but every property is distinct in terms of location, quality (reliability) of tenants, terms of leases, state of repair and scope for development, and some of these characteristics are inter-related; for example, a property in a good location is likely to attract high quality tenants. The financial standing of tenants is important because commercial property leases often have a term of 25 years with provision for *upward*-only rent reviews at five-yearly intervals, so it is possible for leases to create substantial liabilities if open market rents fall during a period of protracted recession and deflation. (If a tenant were to dispose of a lease he would have to make a payment to the new tenant if that tenant had to pay rents above the open market level under the terms of the lease.) Information about individual properties is not available to the public, and buyers of property have to survey a property before committing themselves to a purchase.

Another feature of the commercial property market which distinguishes it from the share market is that there is little, if any, participation in the market by the general public. Taxi drivers and the man on the Clapham omnibus may play a part in stock market bubbles, but not in those in the commercial property market. It does not follow from this that all the participants in the property market are experts: no qualifications or experience are required to set up in the property business and, though most new firms start small (as they do in other trades), in the past some new property firms have been able to grow very rapidly indeed because banks have favoured loans for which property or property developments were available as security. Also, firms in other lines of business own and rent out property. Nevertheless, the important point is that it is not plausible to attribute the booms and crashes in the property market to the 'trading activities of the uninformed' (Seyhun, 1990).

Real rents

One explanation for the long-term growth of real dividends on shares is the earnings on ploughed-back profits, but, as noted in chapter 5, this growth seems to have been surprisingly slow. For property there is no equivalent of ploughed-back profits; the reverse applies, as a part of rents has to be set aside for the depreciation of the property caused by wear and tear and the changing requirements of tenants. As a first approximation no long-term growth of *real* rents might be expected. However, *possible* explanations for growth over the long term are that: (a) increases in site values reflect unique locations which cannot be duplicated because of physical constraints on the availability of land or restrictions imposed by planners or the owners

Table 7.1. *A comparison of nominal returns for bonds, property and equities (before tax and transaction costs)[a]*

From June	To June	25-year Govt. Bonds	FT–Actuaries All Share Index	Property Index	equities win	property wins
		Average annual returns (%)			Periods in which	
1967	1991	9.5	15.9	14.0	√	
1967	1970	− 1.7	10.1	14.5		√
8	1	4.4	6.9	17.0		√
9	2	9.6	17.6	17.7		√
1970	3	6.5	19.1	24.9		√
1	4	− 5.9	− 10.7	11.2		√
2	5	− 1.9	− 9.3	7.1		√
3	6	5.0	− 0.8	2.1		√
4	7	22.1	28.6	14.9	√	
5	8	20.4	24.3	22.0	√	
6	9	18.0	23.6	25.5		√
7	1980	12.4	19.6	22.8		√
8	1	9.6	21.4	19.6	√	
9	2	12.2	15.9	16.2		√
1980	3	22.2	26.5	11.6	√	
1	4	20.6	21.6	8.9	√	
2	5	18.1	29.1	6.9	√	
3	6	13.6	25.4	8.5	√	
4	7	15.9	38.3	10.1	√	
5	8	12.8	20.9	15.3	√	
6	9	7.8	15.6	22.4		√
7	1990	3.7	4.9	19.4		√
8	1	7.1	12.0	8.4	√	

Note: [a] Nominal returns are calculated with income reinvested quarterly. Years to June are used because returns on property are published to June for the period to 1977.
Source: the agents Jones, Lang and Wootton.

on the use of land; and that (b) construction costs could rise faster than retail prices.

Rents, capital values and inflation

Tables 7.1 and 7.2 compare the movements of indices of property[1] and share prices, rents and dividends. The weightings for the JLW Property Index, in terms of 1990 values were: offices, 48%; shops,

Table 7.2. *Asset prices and inflation*

| | A property portfolio | | | | Equities FT-Actuaries All Share Index | | |
| | estimated capital values | | expected real rents[a] for new lettings | actual real rents | share prices | | real dividends[b] |
	nominal	real			nominal	real	
	Indices 1970 = 100 (figures in brackets annual growth rates from 1970)						
June 1970	100	100	100	100	100	100	100
June 1980	288 (11.1)	79 (−2.3)	85 (−1.6)	62 (−4.7)	214 (7.9)	59 (−5.1)	80 (−2.2)
June 1990	555 (9.0)	90 (−0.5)	124 (−2.1)	100 (0.0)	967 (12.0)	142 (1.8)	138 (1.6)
June 1991	487 (7.8)	68 (−1.8)	105 (0.2)	97 (−0.1)	990 (11.5)	137 (1.5)	139 (1.6)
	Percentage changes						
1980–90	93 (6.8)	4 (0.4)	33 (2.9)	47 (3.9)	352 (16.3)	140 (9.2)	72 (5.6)
1980–91	69 (4.9)	−14 (−1.4)	24 (1.9)	57 (4.2)	363 (14.9)	134 (8.0)	74 (5.2)

[a] Estimated current market rents if properties re-let.
[b] An index of notional gross dividends received from a notional investment in the FT–Actuaries All Share Index.
Source: Index of Property Capital Values and Rents: the agents Jones, Lang and Wootton.

31%; industrial property, 20%; and agricultural property, 1%. Two aspects of this Index are noteworthy. Firstly, so far as possible the agents who prepared the Index have excluded gains arising from re-development of property – properties are taken out of the index before development. Properties require substantial renovation from time to time and the cost of such renovation is also excluded from the figures. The manager of a pension fund which held large property estates of high quality estimated that the return from developments, including refurbishments, averaged about 0.5% a year. Secondly, the conventional basis of valuation is used: the value of each property is estimated by valuers on the basis of a deal between a willing buyer and a willing seller. During a property slump, prices realised by a forced seller (who has to sell within, say, several months) may be lower than a valuation based on a transaction between a hypothetical willing buyer and a willing seller. Also, estimates of values of properties which are based on completed transactions for similar properties may lag behind changes in actual prices, especially when prices are falling and there are few transactions to provide benchmarks.

The first row of table 7.1 compares the returns on bonds, equities and property for the period 1967 to 1991 and the remaining rows for periods of three years between 1967 and 1991. Over the period as a whole equities win, showing an average return of 15.9% a year, but the return for property was close, 14%. Over the same period the compound annual rate of increase of retail prices was 9.3%. Property wins in eleven of the three-year periods and equities ten times. (For one period bonds won.) The four highest returns are for equities, but returns on equities were negative for three periods. One qualification to these comparisons is that, as noted earlier, the property valuations are based on estimates for hypothetical transactions between willing buyers and sellers, and valuations may lag behind changes in prices.

Table 7.2 compares movements of capital values of property, share prices, rents and dividends over the period from 1970 to 1991. The first column of figures for property rents are based on estimates of the *expected* rents *if* properties were re-let at current market rents estimated by surveyors. During most of the period since 1970, in the hypothetical event of all properties being re-let at market rents simultaneously, market rents would have fallen because, during periods of rising rents, many tenants benefit from rents set for a term of years when rents were lower than those negotiated for new leases, and this results in them using more space than they would if they were paying higher, contemporary rents.

Over the period 1970 to 1991 as a whole, values of property fell by 1.8% a year in real terms, while expected real rents rose by 0.2% a year (see row 4 of table 7.2). An index of the estimated actual rents

Table 7.3. *Estimated capital values and rents for sectors of the property market, 1980–91*

	Percentage changes			
	in expected rents for new lettings		in values	
	nominal	real	nominal	real
Offices	134	18	61	− 19
Shops	212	57	146	24
Industrial property	126	14	40	− 29
Agricultural	25	− 37	− 10	− 37
Property portfolio	145	23	70	− 15

Note: data for sectors of the market for the period from 1970 to 1980 were not available.
Source: the agents Jones, Lang and Wootton; see Data appendix.

receivable, which lag behind expected rents because rents are renegotiated at intervals of three or more years, is also shown, and this index increased nearly in line with inflation between the years 1970 and 1991. We should recall that over the period 1970 to 1991, real share prices rose at 1.5% a year and real dividends by 1.6% a year. (Data for 1990 are shown in addition to those for 1991 as property values fell between June 1990 and June 1991.)

Over the sub-period 1970 to 1980, which includes the period of very rapid inflation, expected real rents, actual real rents and real dividends fell by 1.6%, 4.7% and 2.2% a year (see row 2 of table 7.2). Over the same period, 1970 to 1980, property was a noticeably better inflation hedge than equities, real property values fell by 2.3% a year while the prices of equities fell by 5.1% a year in real terms. Turning to the period 1980 to 1991, both real share prices and dividends rose very rapidly and faster than real property prices and rents (see row 6 of table 7.2).[2]

Our conclusions so far are that over the period 1970 to 1990, the capital values of property very nearly kept pace with inflation but property values did not move closely in step with retail prices. In 1991 and 1992 property prices fell sharply. The results shown for the composite commercial property index used so far fracture when the changes in the components of the indices are examined. These are shown in table 7.3. In real terms expected rents for newly let shops increased by 57%, while rents for agricultural property fell by 37% between June 1980 and June 1991. One of the most striking features here is that, while the real capital values of shops increased by 24%, the value of agricultural property fell by 37% and industrial property by 29%.

Office property

After a spectacular boom during the early 1970s the property market collapsed in 1974 – simultaneously with a collapse in share prices. Controls on commercial property rents imposed by the Labour Government as a part of its incomes and prices policy contributed to this collapse. During the late 1980s, another property boom led by the London office market developed and was followed by a sharp set-back, and disarray in the market, in 1990. Figure 7.1 shows the movement of office rents for new lettings in *real* terms; the index of rents is set equal to 100 at the beginning of *each* period. The graph distinguishes two booms in real rents and shows the movements of real rents during the period between the two booms. Real rents rose steeply between 1970 and 1974 and in 1987 and 1988; they fell from 1974 until 1978, from 1979 until 1985, and in 1990 and 1991.

A recipe for unstable prices in a market is for total demand and/or supply not to be responsive to changes in prices; for office space the nature of supply is an important explanation for the booms and busts. In the short run, say, three years or so, the supply of new office space is inelastic. An expert on planning estimated that it takes about two years to obtain planning permission for a substantial new office block in London and a further two years to build it. During the boom at the end of the 1980s there was some tendency for the period required to obtain planning permission and the period for construction to increase.[3] Another factor making for inelastic supply is that some property companies stick to their long-term development plans; they plan up to ten years ahead to synchronise the termination of leases for property to be redeveloped. Over a period of from three to ten years there is increasing elasticity of supply in response to high real rents. Table 7.4 reports changes in the supply to City of London offices from 1984 to 1991. Between 1985 and mid 1989 rents more than doubled, while the supply of new offices increased from 1988 onwards.

Rents have formed a modest proportion of the total costs of operating an office – of the order of 20% on average – and this has meant that demand is not very flexible in response to rent increases. The practice of fixing rents for periods of five years means that many tenants are sheltered from increases in rents until their rents are renegotiated, and this may delay the response of demand for space. In addition to the inelastic supply and demand, during the 1980s there were increases in demand for office space, especially new offices suitable for the use of

Table 7.4. *The supply of City offices, 1984–91*

	Index of rents for new lettings[a]	Completions[b]	Take-up	Availability at end of year[b]	Percentage of total space vacant
		Million sq. ft			
1984	100	2.1	4.1	4.5	5.6
1985	106	2.7	6.8	3.9	4.9
1986	126	2.8	6.5	2.2	2.3
1987	189	2.5	6.5	3.4	2.4
1988	236	4.1	5.1	4.9	4.4
1989	256	4.3	4.4	10.5	7.9
1990	247	5.3	4.0	13.9	11.2
1991	196	7.1	3.2	16.7	18.0

[a] Index for June of each year.
[b] Units over 5,000 sq. ft net.
Sources: the agents Healey and Baker for rents; the agents Jones, Lang and Wootton for the remainder of the table.

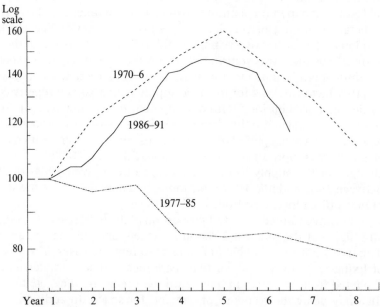

Figure 7.1 Estimated office rents for new lettings in real terms. Source: the agents Jones, Lang and Wootton.

advanced technology. The upward shift in demand for office space for additional staff was caused by the boom in financial services, and new technology led to an increase in the average space required for each employee (to accommodate computers, photocopiers, fax machines, etc.).

Another feature of parts of the financial services industry is that some firms have a very high monetary turnover per employee and at times have achieved, or have expected to obtain, high profits in relation to their costs. Where employees or offices in certain locations have conferred a competitive advantage, these firms have been able to afford fancy salaries and rents, and the fancy rents may have set a benchmark for landlords. In markets where the market clearing price is obscure, such benchmarks can play an important role in price determination for a time. The extent of collaboration and cohesion between landlords or their agents could, for a time, be an important factor in the determination of prices in such markets; one estimate, obtained by the author from a property company, put the share of the five leading firms of estate agents for letting and selling office property in the City as 50% or more.

So far, the fundamental factors influencing the movement of rents have been described, but there are other factors. If, as a result of fundamental forces, or for any other reason, rents and property prices rise, the rise itself may acquire momentum. Instead of choking off demand, higher rents can for a time actually increase demand and reduce effective supply. Some firms which are likely to require space in the future bring forward in time their purchase or renting of space to get ahead of an expected future rise in rents, speculators may take space in the hope of re-letting at a higher rent, and some landlords expecting further increases in rents may not release their property for renting until rents have risen. These actions reinforce the rise in rents and intensify the shortage, but they are probably not a very important influence. More importantly, some participants in the market may form their expectations of future rents by extrapolating relatively recent past changes and base their decisions to develop property on the basis of these expectations. Towards the end of the long 1980s boom this does seem to have happened: if a slowing of the growth of rents had been expected, yields would have risen. In the event, yields on office property did not rise until 1990.

Booms provide benefits for many people while they last, and useful projects which are started during property booms would not be started without such booms. But there is a negative side: resources are concentrated in the construction industry during booms and then left idle; similarly, demand on industries which supply the construction industry has been uneven and led to a waste of resources in those industries. During periods of slack demand the training of employees is cut back.

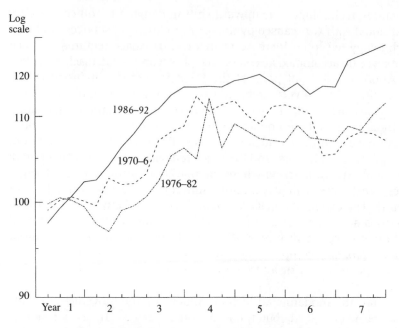

Figure 7.2 Retail sales in volume terms during three booms.
Source: *Economic Trends*, **various issues.**

Also, values of property and the wages of construction workers are bid up during booms, and it is difficult to assess the impact of these price rises on the general rate of inflation. It is particularly noteworthy that booms and crashes occur in the office property market where the general public does not participate and where participants are probably not much influenced by Press comment.

Shop property

Figures 7.2 to 7.5 follow the development of the shop property market through three booms and their aftermath. Again the indices are set at a 100 at the start of each boom. The estimates of yields shown in figure 7.5 are drawn from a different source than the data for figures 7.3 and 7.4, and the two sets of data are not consistent. The data used for figure 7.5 are estimates of yields on prime shop property, actual rents as a percentage of the value of the property; the data for figures 7.3 and 7.4, which were prepared by a different firm of agents, are the expected market rents if rents were negotiated at each point in time the index is prepared (figure 7.3) and estimated capital values (figure 7.4).

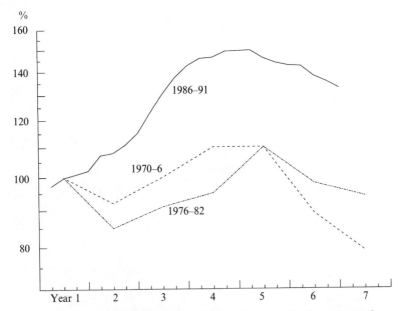

Figure 7.3 Estimated shop rents for new lettings in real terms during three booms. Source: the agents Jones, Lang and Wootten.

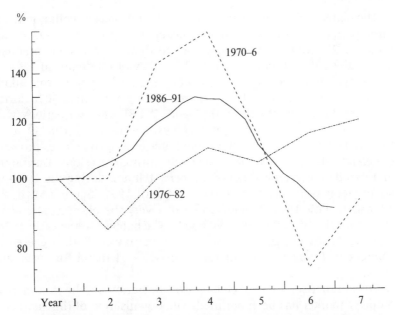

Figure 7.4 Estimated capital values of shops in real terms during three booms. Source: the agents Jones, Lang and Wootten.

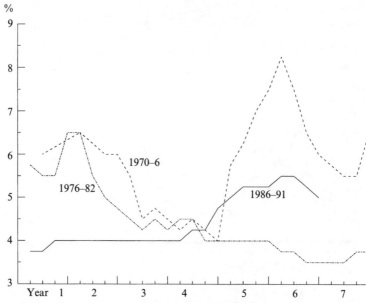

Figure 7.5 Yields on prime shop properties during three booms. Source: the agents Healey and Baker.

The pattern of an increasing volume of retail sales is common to the three periods, though growth was faster during the 1986–92 period (figure 7.2). Another factor forcing up demand for shop premises during the 1986–90 boom was the buoyancy of the financial services sector, with building societies and other financial services firms taking shop space. Estimated real rents increased by no less than 50% during the 1986–90 boom (figure 7.3). Figure 7.4 shows two periods with bubble patterns of rising capital values, 1971–3 and 1987–9, each followed by a burst. Again, these estimates of property values probably understate changes in values, especially during recessions. During the first two booms, yields on shop property fell and during the 1986–90 boom yields were steady at a low level until 1989 (figure 7.5). In the aftermath of the 1971–3 boom, yields rose very sharply and there was a less sharp rise after the 1986–90 boom. The bubbles in the early 1970s and late 1980s in the values of shop property were both triggered by changes in fundamentals: increases in sales, demand for space and rents.

To summarise: in this chapter the operation of the commercial property market has been outlined. The organisation of this market is very different to that of the stock exchange; nevertheless, it too has been subject to bubbles.

Part III

The survey

8 The sample of institutions

One purpose of the survey described in this part of the book was to identify the practices and procedures used by contemporary investors, and to draw out the implications of these practices for the operation of markets.

The survey

The main survey included 18 investment managers, officials of two firms of actuaries and two market makers.[1] The 18 interviews with investment managers were with managers of ten insurance companies, six investment houses and two large pension funds. Insurance companies hold assets in a range of funds: the life fund, the general fund, pension funds which they manage, and unit trust funds. The size of these funds varies greatly – from a few million pounds to more than £10bn. The ten insurance companies, four of which were mutual societies owned by the policy holders, ranged in size from companies with less than £1bn under management to companies with more than £10bn of investments, and together they managed assets totalling more than £50bn. The six investment houses managed investment trusts, unit trusts, pension funds and private accounts: they ranged in size from having £300m to having more than £20bn of funds under management. (Two of the houses, including the smallest house, were described by managers of large houses as 'boutiques' – they were owned by the managers.) The roles and positions within company hierarchies of the officials interviewed varied from the chairman of the investment committee to managers of groups of funds and research groups. Plainly, the investment decisions taken by these managers are important, since the funds are the savings and future pensions of millions of investors.

The sample of financial institutions included in the survey was not random. The main categories of institution not included in the survey were merchant banks and stockbrokers who manage pension funds and investment and unit trusts. Also, there may well have been a bias towards including successful institutions in terms of their investment records. As one purpose of the study was to discover how successful fund managers achieved their good performance, some institutions which were known to have good records and some institutions which were held in high regard by their competitors were selected for inclusion in the survey.

In addition to the main survey in 1990, a few additional meetings were held with fund managers in 1991.

The survey showed that the issues discussed by Keynes in chapter 12 of *The General Theory* are alive and topical, although some of the terminology has changed. The debate about whether the market is driven by assessments based on analysis of known facts and estimates of future profits and dividends – 'fundamentals' (enterprise) – or crowd psychology – 'sentiment' (speculation) – continues.

9 The allocation of investments

The choice of investments

One focus of the discussions was the methods used by the fund managers to allocate investments to various types of asset. There is no controversy about the range of assets from which investments are selected: cash (short-term deposits), bonds (fixed interest securities), index linked bonds, property and equities. For equities, there is a wide range of countries in which to invest, while for fixed interest and property the range is in practice smaller.

From 1923, Keynes was Chairman of the National Mutual Life Company. In his annual report in 1928, Keynes claimed that amongst life offices, the Mutual was pioneering the inclusion of ordinary shares in its portfolio, and in 1927 the proportion rose to 18% of the investment fund. During the 1930s, US as well as UK equities were held for the fund.

In 1990 equities are the largest category of investment held by funds; nevertheless, life funds still hold a significant proportion of their assets in fixed interest securities.[1] At the other end of the range, there are no legal restrictions on unit trusts (including unit trusts operated by insurance companies) being wholly invested in equities. During the 1980s, the proportion of assets invested in equities by pension funds has greatly increased and averaged 68% at the end of 1988 (W M Company, 1990, p. 2). Of the other assets owned by institutions, property is similar to equities in that for the long term it is expected to be inflation-proof. Unusually in 1991, it was seen by managers of some insurance companies as an alternative to bonds. Expectation of slower inflation had increased and office property let to a government department or other secure tenant on the basis of upward-only rent reviews for an unexpired term of 15 to 20 years was seen as being similar to a long-term bond.

Institutions own about two-thirds of the stock of UK equities and the proportion of government bonds they own is higher than this. A market maker estimated that institutional investors, including institutions based overseas, account for more than 80% of turnover in equities, so that inevitably the institutions are competing against each other. Keynes would have included the institutions as professional investors and might have expected such a switch from 'ignorant individuals' to professional investors to lead to greater market stability. Leaving aside the question whether or not professional investors could ever have achieved good investment performance solely by 'forecasting changes in the conventional basis of valuation a short time ahead of the general public', contemporary fund managers as a group cannot do so because the funds they manage are such a large proportion of equities. Also, market makers reported that there was no evidence that collectively the institutional investors made profits *vis-à-vis* private shareholders by trading. A fund manager may seek to beat other fund managers, but fund managers in aggregate are playing a negative sum game. Managers who seek to win by trading incur transaction costs which for some of them lead to a negative result.

Investment managers face uncertainty when deciding how to allocate investment funds. A feature of this uncertainty is that the impact of events which are difficult/impossible to predict can have very large effects on the value of shares. Wars, deep recessions, rapid inflation and Labour Governments are in this category of events (see chapter 5).

Historically, the relative returns on different classes of asset have varied. On average during the post-war period the return on UK equities has been higher than that upon UK fixed-interest securities, bonds and deposits (see chapter 6); during the 1980s, the return on UK equities exceeded the return on both bonds and UK property (see table 9.1). Overseas investments, when valued in sterling, are affected by exchange-rate movements. For five of the years between 1981 and 1990 returns on overseas equities, as measured by world stock indices, exceeded those on UK investments, but they had a negative return of 32.8% in 1990 and a somewhat lower return than UK equities over the full period 1981–90 (see table 9.1).

If they invest a high proportion of their investment funds in equities, fund managers risk at least temporarily, a relatively poor performance if the prices of equities fall. Traditionally, the return on equities is perceived to be more uncertain than that on deposits and bonds, and so a higher return has been expected on them. Moreover, the aggregate value of equities held by institutions is greater than the aggregate of bonds, deposits or property, so again a somewhat higher return might be expected for equities for the institutions to hold a larger stock of equities.

According to neoclassical theorists, investment managers would

Table 9.1. *Nominal gross returns*[a]

		Annual return or average annual return				
	Treasury bills	Bonds over 15 years	Index linked gilts	UK equities	Overseas equities[b]	UK property
1981	15.4	1.6	n.a.	13.7	20.9*	17.1
2	10.0	54.5*	16.6	29.1	32.0	12.7
3	9.0	16.4	0.0	29.1	37.9*	3.9
4	9.3	7.2	5.8	31.9	32.3*	8.2
5	11.5	11.3	0.2	20.4*	12.9	7.5
6	10.9	11.5	5.1	27.4	40.8*	7.0
7	8.4	16.3*	6.2	8.0	−9.3	12.2
8	12.9	9.5	13.0	11.5	31.0*	25.6
9	15.0	5.7	14.3	36.1*	31.5	30.8
1990	13.5*	4.2	3.9	−9.7	−32.8	9.2
1981–90	11.6	13.0	7.2[c]	19.0*	17.1	13.1

Notes: [a] Gross returns include capital appreciation and gross income before tax and transaction costs.
[b] Morgan Stanley World Index to 1987. FT–Actuaries World Index from 1987.
[c] Average for 1982–90.
* Category of investment with the highest return in each year.
Sources: Economic Trends and WM Company, 1990.

place probabilities on all possible outcomes and would optimise in the sense that they would survey and use all the information available to them. In practice, they do *not* place probabilities on all possible outcomes, and there are constraints on the allocation of assets – which are considered next.

Constraints on the selection of investments

There are legal constraints on the selections of investments, and the tightness of these constraints varies. Managers of life funds consider that their selection of investments is limited by the restrictions placed on them by actuaries. Actuaries have to 'sign off' insurance funds: they have to certify the solvency of the funds each year, and thus they are influential in determining the investment policy of companies. The large insurance companies *employ* actuaries who 'sign off' their funds, while smaller companies use independent firms of actuaries.

Actuaries' valuations of both liabilities and assets are conservative: they tend to exaggerate liabilities and take a cautious view of the value of assets. They consider the effects of such eventualities as a fall in the prices of equities of 50% and rapid inflation on the solvency of insurance funds. So far as is possible, actuaries have to ensure that whatever unexpected events occur insurance companies and pension funds will be solvent.

Actuaries

Actuaries acknowledge that assessing the future return on investments is subject to uncertainty. They face difficult choices in protecting the interests of beneficiaries; if they could expect the future to be a replay of the recent past with continuous inflation at varying rates and without a catastrophic recession, then they would authorise heavy commitment to equity/real assets – ordinary shares and property. But they cannot be sure, so they have to consider the effects of a future with, say, zero inflation or with a very deep and protracted recession. For investors, including pensioners who have contracted to receive payment(s) fixed in money terms, actuaries ensure that investments in government bonds or other assets will enable companies to meet their commitments. In part, the decisions of actuaries are based on the practices of funds, and they give similar advice to all the funds they deal with. In the past, actuaries have advocated and insisted that life funds hold substantial fixed interest or cash deposits. Although there are circumstances where the holding of bonds and/or deposits can be justified – where liabilities are fixed in money – the effects of such holdings for much of the period between 1960 and 1990 – to reduce returns – are shown in chapter 6. In practice, managers of insurance funds aim to maintain the proportion of fixed interest and cash in their portfolios at least a little above the minimum set by actuaries.

Many pensions are linked to contributors' final salaries, not fixed in money terms before retirement, and have at least an element of index-linking after retirement. In recent years, actuaries have advocated that pension funds hold a substantial proportion of their funds in equities, because the long-term movement of equity prices and wages to which pensions are now linked have been correlated. Such extrapolation of relationships calculated from past data implicitly assumes the future will be like the past. Legal and actuarial constraints have not limited investment in equities and property by pension funds: 90% of some pension funds are invested in these assets. To compete with unit trusts, life insurance companies have moved away from guaranteeing to pay a fixed sum at the maturity of policies to paying bonuses which depend upon their achieved investment performance. These policies have enabled insurance companies to invest a larger proportion of funds in equities and property and less in bonds and deposits.

The endowment

The extent of the endowment, or reserves, of insurance companies and the pattern of their liabilities constrain their investment policy. For example, a mutual fund with a large endowment could invest all of its general fund and/or funds held to pay annuities in equities, because it could cover its liabilities out of its reserves if equity prices fell. A new insurance company writing general insurance would be more constrained. It would have few reserves and would have to take account of a possible fall in the price of equities in general and the effects on prices of particular shares if the company was a forced seller of its holdings to meet its liabilities. The extent of the free reserves of an insurance company (that is, reserves which have not been committed to bonuses) is a factor limiting overseas investment: certain companies considered that their overseas investments should not exceed their free reserves, the implication being that in the very unlikely event of the overseas investments being wiped out, the companies' liabilities would not exceed their assets.

Other constraints

Some of the restraints on managers are more idiosyncratic. The trade union representatives on the board of trustees of one pension fund had restricted its overseas equity investment to 10% of the fund; trustees of two pension funds excluded any dealing in options or currency hedging – the investment managers could hold overseas equities but they could not hold cash in overseas currencies or hedge overseas investments by selling foreign currencies for forward delivery. Some insurance companies make forward purchases and sales using futures and they also use options. None of the funds managed by the investment managers interviewed entered into short sales of individual shares (sales of shares which the fund did not own) because the liabilities on such sales would be 'unlimited', but they did enter into futures contracts to sell shares. In a sense, the restriction on short sales seems irrational, because a fund would not incur substantial risks by short sales limited to a small proportion of the fund's assets. Certain institutions maintain lists of companies whose chairmen or chief executives are considered untrustworthy and in which the institutions will not invest however alluring the prospects for the companies may appear. Twenty companies were included on such a list held by one investment house.

Fund managers also debate the interpretation of trust deeds and the instructions of pension fund trustees. An investment manager of an insurance company rightly emphasised risk spreading for policy holders. In contrast, the managers of specialised unit trusts may assume that investors are taking account of risks when they invest in the trusts and that the function of the fund managers is not risk spreading. Taking a unit trust for investment in North American equities as an example, the manager has several options. He has a choice whether to hold North American equities, or cash, or a combination of both, and, if he holds North American equities, he can hedge these dollar assets if he expects sterling to rise relative to the dollar. Some managers reason that investors in such a trust will expect to have their investment in North American equities and that they will not expect the dollar investments to be hedged. At one investment house the policy for its unit trusts was for liquidity not to exceed 5% of the fund and to hedge currencies for funds invested overseas only in exceptional circumstances. Some managers say investors expect a fund manager to do whatever he considers necessary within the formal constraints imposed by the trust deed, including going liquid or hedging, to maximise the return on investments in the unit trust. The extent of the freedom to select investments varies between unit trusts: some general trusts can invest in a range of international markets as well as UK gilts and equities.

The perceived expectations of customers was another constraint on insurance companies. One investment manager commented, 'customers do not expect us to deviate from the pack' and 'we must live within our image'; an investment manager of another insurance company said he did not know what customers expected. This works another way: some insurance companies and investment houses sell themselves in terms of having a particular style or approach to management. For example, one insurance company operated a cautious asset allocation policy – it did not switch in and out of equities – and this policy was attractive to the trustees of some pension funds. The investment manager of another insurance company made presentations to pension fund trustees extolling his aggressive approach to investment which involved large changes in liquidity and a rapid turnover of shares.

The tensions faced by investment managers occur because of the pressure to improve performance relative to other investment houses by adopting an adventurous investment policy, the constraints imposed by actuaries and trustees, and the risks of a relatively poor performance associated with an adventurous or distinctive investment policy.

Procedure

Decisions on asset allocation are usually taken by a very small number of managers at all the companies. Estimates were obtained from fund managers that between four and seven key positive decisions on asset allocation are taken for funds in a typical year. Many more passive decisions – decisions not to act or change policy – are made.

There were differences of emphasis between the procedures used by insurance companies and those used by investment houses and we shall start by describing the procedures used by large insurance companies. The allocation of investments is determined at quarterly or monthly meetings of investment committees, and the following elements were common to the procedures used by the companies (though details varied).

1. A paper forecasting the development of the UK, US, Japanese and EEC economies is tabled at the meetings. The forecasts are culled from published forecasts, focus on a time horizon of one to two years, and include forecasts of growth rates of GDP, inflation rates, etc. One company had developed its own composite index to indicate the movement of an economy. Another company forecast alternative scenarios and attached tentative probabilities to the scenarios, while a third company used the London Business School forecast, but examined forecasts which were markedly at variance with it to see why they differed. The economic forecasts are used to forecast the growth of aggregate company profits and dividends for the ensuing two years.

2. Forecasts are made of the expected return in money terms on each category of investment during the next 12 months. When estimating the return on bonds for each country the following influences are considered:

(i)   the expected rate of inflation (for example, at the time of the interviews the changes in Eastern Europe were projected to lead to an increase in the rate of inflation in Germany);
(ii) the borrowing requirement of the government;
(iii) investor preferences – these preferences take account of the political situation in the country and questions such as: Will Japanese investors go on investing in US bonds? (In brief, this is an example of 'the beauty contest' approach.)

Forecasts for bond yields are set out first, perhaps because of their traditional importance and because forecasts of returns on bonds can be made with fewer assumptions and projections than are required to forecast returns on equities.

The forecasts of returns for each category of investment usually take the form of point estimates, not ranges; at one house they were referred to as our 'guesses of total returns'.[2] The forecasts of returns made up of dividends and capital appreciation are made by the analysts and/or fund managers responsible for investment in each category of investment: UK fixed interest, UK equities, US fixed interest, US equities, other European markets, Pacific markets. A principal objective of the meetings is to determine an *ordering* for the expected returns in different markets as a basis for allocating funds.

At these meetings an attempt is made to foresee what recent or new information will move the market, or sectors of the market. Apart from assessing the impact of individual items of news, an attempt is made to assess whether all the good/bad news has been discounted and whether the balance of new information will be good or bad for the market. Are institutions fully invested? Is there any evidence of a bubble, such as borrowing to buy shares and buying by people who do not normally buy shares and who have been attracted by the possibility of making capital gains? For one company the key paper considered at the quarterly investment policy committee meetings described the assumptions the manager made about economic and political developments and their implications. The assumptions for this paper were considered to be crucial and they were set out in such a way that the non-executive directors on the committee could see how the conclusions were reached.

The extent to which decision taking on asset allocation is concentrated varies. In some cases one individual took the decisions and the roles of other members of the committee were to act as a check and to provide advice. In other cases a more collegiate approach was used. The degree to which committee decisions are binding also varies; at one insurance company a committee decision to move into UK equities would be implemented in roughly equal instalments over a three-month period whatever the short-run changes in the market. At two other insurance companies, committee decisions about asset allocation would be overturned the next day if circumstances changed.

There is an absence of long-term projections despite the fact that the 'fundamental' determinant of the price of equities is the future stream of dividends over many years. One insurance company did make outline projections to the year 2000. They 'put a finger in the air' and said the yield on bonds will be 9% in the year 2000 and that the underlying annual rate of inflation will be 5%. The return on investment by companies will be maintained at 15-16% in money terms and retention ratios will remain around 50%. In the year 2000 the yield on equities will be 4% and shares will have risen by 142% in money terms from their February 1990 level. One reason why such projections are rare may be that in most years they would not vary very much from the previous year. Another explanation given by a manager of an insurance company was that there was 'not much point in looking beyond 12 months because we do not know what will happen'.

In contrast to the detailed formal procedures and detailed information used by the large insurance companies, a medium-to-large insurance company held investment policy meetings at intervals of two weeks. The papers for each meeting included a one-and-a-half page review for each major economy and an assessment of a similar length describing the state of each stock market. At one of the two smallest of the insurance companies included in the sample, the investment manager submitted a paper for the quarterly investment committees. The paper included a summary of the decisions taken at the previous meeting, a report on investments made since the last meeting and explanations for changes in the plans formulated at that meeting. This manager shied away from giving quantitative estimates of expected returns. At the second small insurance company, which was owned by an overseas-based insurance company, and at a medium-sized insurance company the procedures were also less formal and detailed than those used by the large companies and there was less distinction between regular monthly meetings and quarterly policy meetings.

At the investment houses, policy decisions seemed to be made at more frequent intervals. At one house the policy committee met weekly and considered a relatively brief paper which was used as a basis for policy discussions. Investment allocation evolved, rather than being set at quarterly meetings. The smallest investment house presented meetings of the trustees of the pension fund it managed with a quarterly report on the state of the market, the performance of the fund and its plans without any detailed forecasts.

Interpretation of evidence and information

Much of the information relevant to the market is available to all fund managers. It is the interpretation of, and the decisions made as a result of the differing interpretations which vary. This can be illustrated by two interviews carried out on the same day. One manager commented that fixed interest investments were no longer 'normal investments' for a pension fund; at the following interview a manager said his company was considering the question whether fixed interest holdings should be increased at least temporarily because the government was committed to reducing the rate of inflation, the recession was reducing profits and a reduction in short-term interest rates to revive the economy would increase bond prices. The option to switch back into equities would always be open.

Probabilities

Generally, the procedures used by all the managers were far removed from making *quantitative* estimates of *all possible* economic outcomes and dividend flows as a basis for decision taking. The attempt by one insurance company to estimate tentative probabilities for alternative scenarios has been noted. One manager was willing to put probabilities on most conceivable eventualities; for example, he considered there was a 15% chance of a major world recession during the 1990s, but he had not increased liquidity in response to this assessment. An example of the use of probabilities was provided by another manager. In 1988 he had taken the view that the rate of inflation would rise to about 8% by 1990 and considered the chance of the rate being below the 5 or 6% consensus forecast which was in the market (already reflected in prices) to be very low. So he bet on what he considered the most likely outcome, faster inflation, by buying index-linked gilts.

Although most managers do not make formal estimates of probabilities, it is possible that they do make intuitive assessments of probabilities of major events. For example, they could assess the chances of a deep world recession or persistent rapid inflation or a major war occurring during the 1900s to be low or very low. If an incident occurs which changes such expectations, the effect on stock prices could be dramatic, reflecting the deterioration in the expected growth of real profits and real dividends. Historically, deep world recessions, major wars and rapid inflation have had damaging effects on the growth of dividends and share prices in real terms at least in the short and medium term (see chapter 5).

If a fund manager believes there is a 10% chance of a major world recession sometime during the 1990s and that if this occurs equity prices will fall sharply, what effect does and should this have on asset allocation? If he adds to liquidity and the recession does not occur (which he perceives to be the most likely outcome) he will underperform relative to competitors and lose business, so he is likely to ignore the possibility of a major recession. The investment decision is likely to be the same whether the chances of a major world recession occurring sometime during the 1990s are reckoned to be 1, 10 or 20%, so there would not be much point in refining estimates of the probability of a major recession if the probability was reckoned to be low, even if it were possible to make such estimates. The manager will hope that he can spot the onset of any recession and reallocate his investments before it happens.

The alternative view expressed by one fund manager was that 'many things cannot be quantified' – such as the chances of wars and oil shocks occurring – so they are ignored. Again, there were echoes of an observation made by Keynes, that investors assume that the present is a 'serviceable guide to the future'. The chance of another stock market crash was likened to the chance of a pedestrian being knocked down by a car – it could be ignored.

In view of the record of real dividend and share price movements reported in chapter 5, it is interesting to note that many fund managers considered the future election of a Labour Government would not make much long-term difference to the market.

Competition and assessment

Fund managers compete with each other, and they lose business if their investment performance is relatively weak. Fund managers considered that competition had increased. Investors now have a wide range of investments from which to select and this puts pressure on managers of traditional types of funds (for example, those selling life insurance) to achieve good performance. There is intense competition to manage pension funds, and managers believe that the trustees of pension funds rely upon performance tables when deciding upon potential managers to interview for appointments. One obvious way to limit any divergence in performance is to match the investment distribution of competing funds. Here there is a clear echo from Keynes's writings – the fund managers are in effect forced back on the judgement of others, they 'conform with the behaviour . . . of the average'.

League tables are prepared of the performance of fund managers and targets are set for managers in terms of these league tables or market indices: a pension fund manager may be given the objective of being in the top half or top quartile of the W M Company's league table of the performance of pension funds. According to the Bank of England's survey of fund managers, 'most of the merchant banks and independent fund managers thought that their performance was viewed over a rolling three-year period . . . There was some indication that a few pension fund trustees, particularly those for smaller funds, reacted to poor performance over an even shorter period' (Bank of England, 1987, p. 53).[3]

In practice, if a manager has a continuously good record he is unlikely to be dislodged but, as shown in chapter 14 below, even successful managers have 'off' years when their systems (such as investing in small companies or shares with higher than average yields) fail or they misjudge market trends. Some of the trustees or committee members who appoint a manager may have reasons for favouring other managers and take advantage of such a temporary lapse in performance: long-term performance is not necessarily the only criterion.

The extent to which funds are exposed to competition varies; life funds are judged by their performance in providing bonuses, but unit trusts are judged on their short-term performance relative to their sector of the unit trust market. Although insurance companies publish annual accounts, it is difficult to make comparisons of overall investment performance from these because the pattern of their policies and liabilities varies, and so their annual declarations of bonuses are a focus of attention; in the long term, bonuses reflect the investment performance of an insurance company but for a period of years a company can camouflage its performance by using its reserves. Insurance companies do manage unit trusts and pension funds whose records are available for comparison.

Prices and hence performance comparisons are available on a daily basis for unit trusts. Many units are sold through intermediaries who have a vested interest in changing investments because they receive a commission on purchases, and failure compounds itself; if a unit trust has to liquidate units and sells parts of its holdings, this will tend to push down prices of the investments it holds and further weaken performance. Also, its best investments, in terms of prospects, may be the most marketable, so the managers are tempted to sell these first and hold the ones which may prove to be duds. The relative performance of the high profile unit trusts rubs off onto the other business of the fund managers, including management of pension funds and life business – if its unit trusts perform relatively badly it makes for greater difficulty in obtaining management contracts for pension funds and for selling life insurance contracts. The extent to which funds compete on performance varies. Large companies can employ a large sales force and advertise without focusing on their relative record, while a small investment house may have to rely almost exclusively on its past performance to attract business. At least in the past, some insurance companies competed by providing large commissions to third parties who introduced business.

The trade off between relative performance and asset allocation has been noted. As a fund manager varies the distribution of his investments from that of his competitors he increases the chance of outperforming them, but he also increases the margin by which he may lag their performance. It is very important to avoid a *relatively* bad performance. One manager used a *benchmark* to limit his risk. The distribution of investments for 30 competing funds was averaged; the manager allowed investments in UK equities, which made up about 50% of the fund, to vary by ten percentage points from the average, and the other categories of asset, such as fixed interest bonds, to vary by five percentage points. This rule was an innovation which resulted from the 1987 crash. Another insurance company followed a similar rule except that each category of investment could be varied by up to eight percentage points from the average for the funds with which it made comparisons.

Details of the investments held by each unit trust are published twice a year, but the information is up to two months out of date when it is published. It may seem surprising that fund managers are willing to divulge the information, but managers obtain more up-to-date information about the allocation of investments by other unit trusts by asking for it by telephone from the managers of the other trusts, either openly swapping information about the allocation of investments or by pretending to be a potential investor interested in the investment policy of the trust. For pension funds, 'hard' information about the performance of other funds is available about two weeks after the end of each quarter; in between quarterly reports, managers can get 'soft' information from brokers about changes in asset allocation by other pension funds.

The proprietor of the smallest investment house claimed that he ignored the asset distribution of other managers of pension funds and unit trusts. This house, as well as one of the pension funds which provided information for the study, had above-average performance in recent years. The pension fund had outperformed the average for pension funds by holding more than average Japanese equities and property. An investment manager whose funds outperform the average has, of course, more freedom to depart from the average distribution. If he has a subsequent period of poor performance he can average his record; this is an example of success providing possible opportunities for further success. However, the managers of two funds whose performance had greatly improved claimed that their leading or good positions in a pension funds league table had not altered their approach or investments; in these cases, success enabled managers to continue with a successful strategy. (In one case the reason for good performance in 1990, relatively low holdings of equities and larger holdings of fixed interest and property, led to relatively weak performance in 1991.) At a large insurance company recent underperformance of the portfolio of UK equities relative to the indices was said to have made fund managers receptive to the introduction of more sophisticated risk analysis of portfolios.

Readers may be curious as to why so many funds can advertise that they have a *relatively* good report. It is therefore noteworthy that relative performance changes through time and that each manager uses the period(s) during which his house has a good performance as the basis for publicity. In this sense there can be more than one winner.

The other 'boutique' also ignored the allocation of funds made by other investors; it took large bets and was not concerned if its allocation varied from that of other firms. However, there was a tie to the allocation of funds made by other houses: if the boutique believed there were good prospects for a market on the basis of fundamentals (the expected short-term growth of output of an economy and company profits) it tried to assess whether this was already in prices. In effect, the boutique was trying to be a step ahead of the herd by analysing economic fundamentals for countries.

One manager commented, 'we certainly have to take a conscious view of what other people think'. He considered investment was a fashion 'business'; in the short term the sentiment of other market participants was important. Sometimes the company wanted to swim with the tide and sometimes to go against it. However, in further discussion it became clear that the manager was not trying to pick out the next fad or fashion, but was looking for valuations based on assessments which did not conform to his own assessment of fundamentals. He aimed to take advantage of bubbles, fads and fashions by anticipating their collapse and the triumph of fundamentals; he aimed to be ahead of the pack.

It was clear from the discussions that for most fund managers the allocation of investments by competitors was a crucial influence in determining their allocation. One manager said his team considered fundamentals when making its decisions on allocation; they 'did what they thought was right', and ignored the pack, but he admitted that if the company had invested 15% in Europe compared to the pack investing 10%, there would be little point in increasing the size of its bet: the company would win – relative to the others – if European shares did well. Fund managers were willing to take 'bets'; a surprising example was a company which in a single afternoon had hedged all its US investments against an expected fall in the dollar. Nor has the pressure to conform to the average prevented large changes in the composition of funds through time. During the 1980s holdings of overseas equities increased, and the proportion of fixed interest securities in portfolios declined. Managers have scope for changing their asset allocation but conforming to the average may have slowed changes. This may or may not have contributed to stability of prices.

A manager of one investment house admitted to being 'locked into' the consensus view for the allocation of assets for the pension funds it managed. A manager of another investment house illustrated the dilemmas when faced with the property bubble during the early 1970s and the share market during the pre-crash period in 1987. If the house was to match the performance of its competitors it had to stay in the market during the bubbles, even though, judged on fundamentals, prices were reckoned to be too high. The aim was to sell out just before the crash and not be left holding property or shares during it, but this was very difficult to achieve.

One view of a fund manager replicating the asset distribution of other funds is that this system limits the extent of any failure to match the performance of other funds. Another viewpoint is that, as the institutions are the principal investors, their investment decisions are likely to move the market, so one recipe for success is to invest with the herd of institutions, preferably at the front end. Here again there is an echo from Keynes: a modern version of the beauty contest is for fund managers to guess what other managers are doing *or will do next*.

Liquidity

An important aspect of asset allocation is decisions on liquidity. In the 1920s and 1930s, liquidity preference related to the choice between holding bonds or equities and cash or deposits. By the 1980s, the principal decisions about liquidity related to movements between equities and cash deposits, but movements from fixed interest to cash can still be quantitatively important. (A manager of a fund may decide to sell all his fixed interest holdings and hold cash on deposit if he expects bond prices to fall. He is very unlikely to sell all his equity holdings if he expects a fall in equity prices.) As with other investment decisions, investment managers decide to increase liquidity when they expect the return on cash deposits to exceed that on equities or bonds. During the summer of 1990, interest rates on deposits were about 15% per annum and the dividend yield on equities about 5%, so prices of equities had to rise by more than 10% per annum to outperform deposits. If a manager decided equities were unlikely to beat this target he would incur charges by switching, but managers may avoid these by simply holding back the inflow of cash from new contributions or the sale of additional units and the proceeds of takeovers.

For the large insurance companies changes in liquidity are muted because their managers believe they cannot change their liquidity without moving the market and because 'they must live within their image'. One large insurance company would not allow liquidity to go much over 10%, but the level of liquidity varied between its funds. The fund management division of a stockbroker also gave 10% as the upper limit for liquidity. At the time of the interviews a medium-sized company had 14% of its funds in cash and 10% in bonds, while a medium-sized insurance company had 14% of its funds in cash and 10% in bonds. Another medium-sized to large insurance company had liquidity of 7%, which it considered a high level of liquidity. This company had allowed liquidity to build up during the year without actually selling any shares to increase liquidity.

At the time most of the interviews took place, July 1990, both of the smaller insurance companies had relatively high levels of liquidity on their high profile funds: 16% and 23%. The first company had raised its liquidity in February 1990 and had not reduced it when share prices rose later in the year. One of the small independent investment houses built up the liquidity of the pension fund it managed to 40% in March 1990 but re-entered the market in April and May 1990 when prices increased.

The existence of substantial liquidity among the institutions has implications for market stability. While some of the smaller institutions alter their liquidity and this could be destabilising, larger institutions could destabilise the market by allowing their liquidity to build up or run down, especially if they acted together. The managers of large funds see variations in their liquidity as a means of averaging the cost of the equities they acquire – stabilising, rather than destabilising, the market. The strategy of one investment manager was 'to spot when market movements were exaggerated'. If houses are to act contrary to the market, at times they have to build up liquidity.

Hedging currencies and new financial instruments

Currency hedging, share options and futures contracts provide flexibility for asset allocation. Although funds do hedge currencies, most managers acknowledge that it is difficult to get currencies right – more difficult than market allocation or share selection. For most managers, activity in options and futures markets was limited. Sometimes they write (sell) put options when they wish to buy the shares of a company. (A put option gives the buyer the right to sell the share at a stated price within a specified period. For newly issued options the nominated price is usually close to the current market price). If, as expected by the writer of the option, the price of the shares rises, the put option will not be exercised and the profit on the option when it expires will reduce the effective costs of purchases of the shares. Futures are used to commit expected future inflows early when the market is expected to rise but also by certain companies to take bets on expected movements of prices.

Generally, the managers did not separate expected share market and exchange rate movements. They did not decide to invest in equities in a market such as Japan or the USA and simultaneously hedge to another currency.

Benchmarks

There is a range of market indicators used by managers to assess the state of the market. The average price earnings (P/E) ratio for the market is particularly important: investment managers do not expect it to diverge widely from its historical range. Also, the ratio of the dividend and earnings yields to the yield on bonds is closely monitored.[4] The US reverse yield gap rose with an increase in bond yields in advance of the crash in 1987; and the 1990 share price collapse in Tokyo was preceded by a rise in the Japanese reverse yield gap, again triggered by rising bond yields. (A fall in bond prices and an increase in bond yields does not always lead to a fall in equity prices.) Similarly, the dividend yield on equities is important; one manager used it as a basis for a rule: consider selling if the expected dividend yield (expected dividends next year as a percentage of the current price) is below 4% and buy if it is above 6%. Increases in dividends more than one year ahead were not considered. Likewise, one of the pension funds had followed a rule during 1990 to buy selectively when the FT–SE Index was at, or below, 2,200 and to sell selectively when it was at, or above, 2,400. Another manager commented, 'when equities are ahead of the game we build up liquidity'. Generally, managers attempting to top and tail the market in this way do not buy and sell the same shares. When they consider the market is at a high level within its range, they sell shares of companies about whose prospects they are doubtful and when the market is low they buy the shares of companies whose prospects they consider attractive.

Such benchmarks and rules have important consequences. Firstly, they tend to keep the market *within* its past range and so they damp down fluctuations. Secondly, during much of the post Second World War period the equity market has been undervalued – the average return on equities has been higher than on fixed interest or property (see chapter 6). Adherence to past *P/E* ratios and dividend yields tends to perpetuate this undervaluation and could explain some takeovers.

The share of profits in GDP was another statistic which was monitored. The share of profits in GDP rose during the 1980s; managers questioned whether the rise could continue, and considered the consequences of a slow down. Two investment managers believed that profits could not go on increasing as a proportion of GDP as they had done during the 1980s and that this would put a cap on the rise in equity prices during the 1990s.

Several benchmarks were used to allocate investments between international markets. One benchmark was the valuation of each market during recent years; this has given a relatively heavy weight to Japan and a low weight for Germany because of the high market valuation of Japanese shares relative to the book value of the underlying assets of the companies, and because a larger fraction of German industry is outside the quoted share sector than in the US or the UK. An alternative benchmark was GDP for each country; this reduces the weights for the US, the UK, Switzerland and Sweden below that attributable to market valuations partly because quoted companies in these countries have large overseas investments.

Some of the benchmarks used by companies were less predictable. One of the small investment houses and one pension fund manager considered Hong Kong too risky. It was possible that the entire investment in Hong Kong could be lost. Other funds had substantial investments in Hong Kong. For one company the inflow of contributions and income relative to payments was monitored. The implication was that if this were to be negative it would be a factor requiring the investment managers to seek higher yields on their investments. A manager of a pension fund made a similar point: the fund would not like to get into a position where it had to sell assets to fund a substantial proportion of its expenditure because of uncertainty about share prices.

Certain technical analyses were used; for example, the balance of the number of shares which rose and the number which fell relative to the movement of the market index. If, when the market index rose, there was an excess balance of falls, this was taken as a signal of market weakness.

Conclusions

There are differences in the procedures and investment strategies followed by investment managers. The constraints on the investment policies of fund managers, the practice of matching the asset allocation of competitors and other benchmarks which have been described in this chapter are important influences on the asset allocation decisions of fund managers.

10 Selection of shares

Share picking

So far the main focus of the book has been the returns on classes of investments – equities, bonds, etc.; in this chapter the selection of individual equities is considered. The view of most managers was that market allocation made a more important contribution to performance than stock picking – which could add or subtract 1 or 2% a year to performance. An alternative view was that both asset allocation and share selection would make 1 or 2% difference to performance.

Market allocations are decided by committees or between committee meetings by groups made up of senior managers; stock picking is delegated to individuals and groups responsible for categories of investment and/or separate funds. Individual fund managers are given a good deal of discretion, though the limitations on this discretion vary between companies.[1] In part because of this form of organisation, fund managers and companies do not make a comprehensive evaluation of all the quoted shares available for investment. The larger insurance companies and houses each monitor and evaluate the top 100 or so shares, but outside that range they do not have the resources to evaluate every share. Shares are sifted out on the basis of a few characteristics, or picked out unsystematically or in response to brokers' analyses, news or hunches, and attention is focused on these companies. The shares of some small and, perhaps, medium-sized companies could slip through the net with none of the institutional investors paying attention to them. A possible result of this unsystematic approach is that analysts and fund managers may tend to respond to the same brokers' circulars or news at the same time.

Fund managers monitor the allocation of investments by their competitors, but they do not monitor their share selection to the same extent.

Share selection by a fund

The managers of one fund with substantially more than £1bn invested in UK equities allowed the author to examine the purchases and sales of UK equities made by the fund during a period of four months in the first half of 1990. During the period, the fund sold shares in 30 companies and sales were equal to just under 6% of the portfolio – i.e., at an annual rate of 17% of the total holdings. The sales were not required to pay for benefits. Two of the sales representing nearly 20% of the total by value were made in response to takeover bids. A feature of the sales and purchases was the repeated sales and purchases of certain shares which took place: there were 14 sales of Glaxo and 12 purchases of Dixons. A large fund cannot unload or acquire substantial holdings with a single sale or purchase. The fund sold some of its holding of Glaxo because it was over-weight in the stock and the purchases of Dixons followed sales of the stock earlier at higher prices. Some shares were sold which would fall later in the year, including Coloroll, Midland Bank and Barratt Developments, but shares in Polly Peck and Parkfield were purchased and these companies failed. There were some switches between banks, out of Midland, Barclays and Abbey National and into National Westminster, and between companies making building products, out of Bowater and Blue Circle and into BPB. Most sales and purchases were in different industries, out of pharmaceutical and brewery companies and into electrical engineering, retailing and chemicals. In the short term, these switches between industries were counter-productive because the Gulf crisis and the onset of recession caused sharp falls in electrical engineering and chemical shares later in 1990. The only major company whose shares were bought and sold within the period was Shell.

There are numerous reasons for selling shares including settling liabilities, takeover bids and a perceived deterioration in the relative prospects for a sector or a particular company, unless this is foreseen earlier by other investors. Some shares which appreciate over a long period become over-weight in a portfolio and are trimmed, while other shares are sold to make way for shares which are thought to have better prospects.

Share selection and the size of funds

As already noted, the size of funds managed by the insurance companies varies a great deal, and this affects the extent to which a fund can sell shares. Giant life funds cannot liquidate a large fraction of their equities without pushing the market down in front of the sales (market makers quote prices for limited lines of stock; if a large insurance company starts to sell, the market makers will reduce the prices they quote).[2] Also, life funds have to pay capital gains tax, which inhibits the sale of shares on which substantial capital gains have accrued. Given this difference in the prospects for selling holdings, different *procedures* for share picking might be expected; the life funds might be expected to assess the long-term performance of new acquisitions, while small pension funds exempt from capital gains tax might concentrate on 'in and out' or cyclical stocks. In practice, such distinctions do not apply within insurance companies; similar shares are selected for all the funds except that small funds are likely to hold shares in some smaller companies which are not held in the life fund. Another difference is that a large fund has holdings in more companies, and it may also spread its purchases and sales of shares in a cyclical company over a longer period – not attempting to buy at the bottom and sell at the top. A life fund may invest in venture capital situations which are unsuitable for unit trusts because such holdings cannot be sold quickly.

The proprietor of the smallest investment house took a distinctive view about stock selection. This had been the source of the house's success, though it had also had some success in selecting markets.[3] About 200 meetings a year were held with company managements and particular attention was paid to the management records of the principal managers of companies; these meetings were considered a significant factor in the house's success. The firm had also built up contacts with people knowledgeable about industries, companies and managers. To win, the firm had to select winners; if it invested in ten shares it could hope for five or six winners and only one or two duds. The firm looked for anomalies in the market; sometimes it used systematic analysis – for example, making a survey of all companies with high yields and profits cover for dividends of more than three times. The firm had been notably successful in investing in certain companies which had grown by takeovers and for which the strength of the prices of the companies' shares was integral to their success.

An investment manager who had managed a special situations trust in 1986 and 1987 had used a screening formula to trace shares of small companies which had risen rapidly without the company having announced increased profits or dividends. The purpose of the screening was to discover possible shell companies which new investors were moving into. The companies identified in this way were then analysed and this system was very successful for a time. The proprietor of the smallest investment house and the manager who screened for shell companies were in contact with some managements at frequent intervals. A company which is growing rapidly by takeovers and issuing new shares has frequent contacts with its backers to facilitate the take up of its new shares. It is noteworthy, however, that some of the companies which expanded very fast by takeovers between 1986 and 1988, including Coloroll, British and Commonwealth, and Parkfield, did not stand the test of time. By 1990 they were forced into liquidation by the recession.

Projections of companies' profits

Many fund managers rely upon the investment analysis made by stockbrokers. Generally, brokers quantify projections of profits for a period two years ahead. Stockbrokers and managers focus on this time scale when making forecasts because for many companies forecasting profits beyond two years is difficult. (There are exceptions – for a few companies such as pharmaceutical manufacturers and Marks and Spencer it is considered possible to make longer-term projections because demand for drugs is relatively stable and the companies' positions are protected by patents, and because of Marks and Spencer's strong competitive position in the UK retail market.) As profit projections form the basis for decisions to buy and sell, share prices could become dependent on short-term profit prospects, but it is not easy to assess how far fund managers are tied to the short-term quantitative projections. For companies such as Tesco the short-term profit projections might be seen as indicating trends, but for the cyclical chemical and engineering stocks allowance has to be made for the stage in the cycle when assessing profitability. (The cycles are not, of course, even in terms of duration or amplitude.)[4] Also, the medium-term and long-term prospects for the economies and industries in which companies operate and the extent to which companies are protected from competition by barriers to entry are considered. A manager who emphasised the importance of fundamentals looked for opportunities to be ahead of the pack. In June 1990 he was considering buying shares in companies whose business included house building – he expected the market for new houses to recover in about three years and that the shares of house builders would recover before then.

Contacts with managers

All the investment houses had contacts with managers of companies, but none of them had staff who concentrated on, or made a speciality of, visiting managers of firms. Contacts with managements were either at meetings arranged by brokers for investment managers and analysts, meetings at the companies' establishments, or meetings at individual investment houses. In the case of one insurance company, meetings with managements were arranged towards the end of a sifting process. For example, after screening for shares with consistent profits growth relative to their price/earnings (*P/E*) ratio and studying brokers' reports on the shares identified, the insurance company might arrange to visit 20 firms, but by the time it had sought a meeting there was a 90% chance it would invest in a company; it was a case of checking whether an investment could be made which was justified by information from other sources. It was generally agreed that meetings with managements of small companies were more productive than meetings with managers of companies like BP or ICI. When visiting a small company it is possible to find out the general attitude of management: for example, whether they are more concerned with achieving a good return for shareholders or protecting the interests of employees, their expectations for profits growth and the basis for these expectations. Some of the information provided by managers will be intended to mislead investors: for example, managers of a company with a liquidity problem may conceal it. Also, the implications of the information drawn by fund managers may be different from those intended by the managers providing the information. For example, if the managers of a general chemicals company claim that the company's markets will not be cyclical in future, investors may conclude that the managers are deluding themselves and are making unwise investments. The investment manager of an insurance company gave off-balance-sheet assets and liabilities as an example of the information his company tried to obtain at meetings. But the same manager had found great difficulty in assessing firms developing machinery, even with the benefit of meetings with managers. A fund manager of an insurance company rated contacts with management important: it was possible to assess the chief executive and whether the management was a team or a 'one man band'. (In his guide to *Predicting Corporate Failure*, Argenti (1984) gave an autocratic chief executive as a primary non-financial signal of impending corporate failure.)

Generally, company visits and discussions with managers of companies were not considered a key to successful share picking. The smallest investment house was an exception to this assessment: as noted earlier, this house made an attempt to assess the quality of the management and there was evidence that it had had success in picking out some very successful managers and hence companies in which to invest. Also, an investment house which had large stakes in some companies invited managers of those and various other companies to its offices where they were questioned by its investment managers. It was said this procedure had proved very useful for deciding whether to invest in companies and whether to continue to hold investments. Both these houses had a record of outperforming market indices and most of their competitors. Another house, which declined to be included in the sample and which had an outstanding record, also stressed its contacts with managers in its literature.

Risk analysis

Some institutions used computer programmes designed to analyse risk. These programmes are based on analyses of *past* variability of prices and can be used to indicate how close to market averages *a portfolio* could be expected to perform. They can also be used to provide an indication of the effects of exchange rate changes, interest rate changes, faster inflation, a recession or an oil price shock on a portfolio. Some companies used such programmes as a check; for example, if the programme unexpectedly showed a *portfolio* would perform badly if the exchange rate rose, the managers would analyse the reasons. Another illustration of the use of programmes was to analyse why a portfolio had underperformed the index. Was it made up of companies with higher than average betas during a period when the market was falling? The programmes are used by actuaries when assessing the past performance of funds to check upon the extent to which actual performance is related to the riskiness of a portfolio.

When assessing the prospects for individual companies, statistics such as betas are of very limited utility because analysts use much more information about companies than that encapsulated in such statistics.

Industrial spread

The industrial spread of investment is treated as a second order matter. None of the managers set targets for industrial sectors within UK equities as they did for categories of investments: equities, fixed interest, etc. The prospects for sectors were considered and the composition of portfolios was analysed to assess exposure to sectors. Shares were selected and they 'kept an eye' on the sectoral spread. A manager of an insurance company, who at first claimed that it used no benchmarks to determine asset allocation or share selection, did watch the percentage of investment in oil companies. The oil sector carries a large weight in weighted share indices, and BP and Shell are super giant companies. Some funds have special rules for the percentage of the fund which may be invested in BP and Shell.

Monitoring investments in companies based overseas

With one exception none of the sample of institutions had offices located overseas for analysing markets and companies. One investment house had a fund manager and an assistant in Tokyo. Analysts and fund managers from the UK visited markets for which they were responsible and the institutions used the analyses provided by brokers based overseas. (They rewarded brokers who provided useful information with extra business transactions. One house never bought shares of overseas-based companies through the London market: it bought in overseas markets to reward brokers overseas who provided information.) One company had five managers covering Europe apart from the UK; they were based in the UK but each manager had lived overseas and spent about three months a year in Europe. It was claimed by one house that if they had an office in New York there would have to be nearly as much travelling to cover the USA as if the staff were based in the UK.

Testing the EMH

The mix and complexity of the procedures used by institutional investors to select shares means that direct and simple tests of the EMH do not establish whether the procedures actually used enable houses to outperform the market and contradict the EMH. One form of test is to assess whether the institutions persistently beat the market. The average record of institutions reported in chapter 14 shows that on average they do not outperform the index, though some houses do.

Conclusions

The important, if self-evident, implication of the evidence about share selection is that it is very difficult/impossible to predict the long-term performance of companies. If it were practicable, the large insurance companies would have overseas offices assessing local companies, they would use different procedures for selecting shares for their large long-term funds and they would place more emphasis on the selection of shares.

Nevertheless, some management houses do have a record of outperforming the market and their competitors, and at least in some of these cases meetings with, and information about managers of the companies seem to be an important ingredient in their success.

11 Market makers and views of the market

Market makers

Market makers cover their operating expenses and make their profits from the jobbers' turn (the difference between the prices at which they offer to buy and sell securities) and by taking 'positions' in shares.[1] The manager of the smaller of the two firms of market members which provided information when interviewed for the study reckoned his firm made most of its profits from taking positions, not from the jobbers' turn. This conflicts with the conclusion of another author (Lazar, 1990), that jobbers 'make most of their money by dealing rather than because the value of their holdings appreciated'. Also, the profits of market makers seem to be positively related to stock market turnover and as the aggregate income from the jobbers' turn would be positively related to turnover this supports Lazar's conclusion.

The sum of the positions taken by market makers at any one time represents a very small fraction of their turnover. The sum of the long and short positions taken by one market maker averaged about two or three days turnover,[2] and the net balance of positions was much less than the sum of the long and short positions.[3] When they take a position in a share, market makers generally look to clear it over a week or two rather than months. Random disturbances to prices are likely to occur because of the uneven flow of orders to buy and sell individual stocks, so market makers have to move prices to balance their books. Price fluctuations are an inevitable consequence of spot or liquid markets because of the uneven flow of orders. In addition, the market makers have a vested interest in creating business and, given uncertainty about the value of shares, they can and do create some business by simply moving prices. An increase in the price of a share may trigger extra *purchases* as some market participants infer that someone has favourable information about the company, or that if they delay a purchase the price will be higher still.

Market makers would be expected to have an advantage in information about who is buying and selling shares, and jobbers with a large share of the market have more of this information than firms with a small share.[4] One large jobber had a staff of about 100 people supporting market makers by analysing information about economies and companies, but my impression was that formal information analysis (including information about buyers and sellers) is not the key to successful jobbing. Market feel and *nous* are more important.

Stockbrokers, including both market makers and agency brokers, compete in two main ways.[5] Since the abolition of fixed commissions in 1986 brokers compete on price, providing the best deal for their clients (which depends in part on minimising their costs).[6] Stockbrokers also compete by providing services to their customers, a form of competition which increases costs. In a rough and ready way fund managers pay brokers for the information and analyses they provide by allocating business to them. Since the Big Bang changes which were outlined in chapter 1 were introduced in 1986, there has been a conflict between minimising costs and providing services which clients do not pay for directly. The present system probably favours the smaller insurance companies and fund management groups, as they would be at a greater handicap in replacing the information they get from brokers.

Market making by fund managers

The managers of funds do not see themselves as market makers; certainly they do not set prices at which they are obliged to trade stocks. Yet, although they do not make markets in the strict sense that they announce prices at which they are obliged to deal, fund managers do participate in market making. A sense in which one insurance company considered it helped make markets was that it would buy shares with a view to reselling within two weeks or so. The example of this sort of intervention given was of a recent acquisition of a food manufacturer by a quoted company which changed the nature of the acquiring company. When the insurance company bought the shares it believed that the market had not acknowledged this change in the price of the acquiring company's shares. The heavy turnover of shares by many funds suggests this company is not exceptional.

One explanation for the high turnover of shares is that fund managers play a part in making the market work; they respond to price signals set by market makers which are designed to balance trade in shares. The point can be put another way: if fund managers held stocks long term and did not respond to short-term price movements, fluctuations in share prices might well be greater. In fact, from the national point of view, a justification for the high turnover of shares is that it makes possible informed share valuations, but this does not necessarily ensure profits for the operators. The financial institutions and other market participants have an interest in the maintenance of a market with such valuations which would not exist if trading were limited by, for example, most participants buying index-linked funds. Informed share valuations are desirable for investors when companies raise additional capital and when investors wish to sell shares to meet liabilities or buy other assets. However, most of the fund managers see their role as investors rather than as assisting market making. (One senior manager put it this way: if one of his managers bought for 220 on Monday and sold for 225 on Friday he would want to have an explanation.)

There is a serious and important qualification to the view that increased trading results in informed valuations: institutions act as a herd. The reasons for this are varied and sometimes arise from fund managers accepting the same advice from brokers, following each other (see chapter 9) or many of them simultaneously interpreting or misinterpreting the new information they peruse. The fact that the variability in the price of shares in smaller companies (which are relatively little traded) is no greater than for the shares of large companies (for which there is vastly more trade) is an indication that trading does not necessarily dampen fluctuations in prices.

The size of the jobbers' turn is inversely related to the turnover of shares, and this is approximately proportional to the capitalisation of companies. For very large companies such as British Telecom the jobbers' turn is less than 0.5%, while for very small companies whose shares are traded infrequently, the turn can be as much as 10%. If there were less turnover in UK shares, there would be fewer market makers and/or the market makers would have smaller operations and the jobbers' turn might well be somewhat higher; one way or another, the cost of market making has to be recouped.

Views of the market

Views of the market varied between the fund managers. One view in line with the EMH was that all existing information was in the market; new information and shocks would change prices so the function of managers was to assess whether, on balance, new information was likely to lead to an increase in prices or to a fall – this manager viewed fundamentals as important. At the other extreme, a fund manager who was disparaging of the investment record of those managers who relied on fundamentals stressed the importance of being able to judge which way the market was moving. In similar vein, an actuary believed that managers tried to foresee the next 'theme' in the market. This interview took place soon after the market had risen in response to the government announcing that it planned to join the ERM. One manager took a more comprehensive view; fundamentals (the expected profits and dividends paid by companies) set the level of the market within a band of 20% on either side and sentiment (confidence) determined the position within that band. These views suggest there is no trustworthy level for the market set by fundamentals because so much of the information needed to assess the fundamental value of shares is unknowable; the long-term return on equities is uncertain, but some outcomes are considered by managers to be more likely than others. Interestingly, investment managers considered the Japanese market to be valued on a *different basis*, with much higher *P/E* ratios and lower dividend yields. Again this suggests that fundamentals do not dictate a unique price level though legal, institutional or traditional barriers to movements of capital could create different bases for valuations between countries.

Conclusion

The influence market makers exert on prices is difficult to assess. As their holdings are very small relative to the total shares in issue and as they turn over their holdings of shares rapidly, their influence on prices in the medium to longer term should be small. However, because of the uncertainty about the real value of shares and because of noise traders, their influence on the general level of prices should be significant in the short term. For shares of companies for which turnover is low, the decisions of market makers on pricing can be significant over periods of several months or longer.

12 Competition between fund managers and investment strategies

The management of portfolios is a highly competitive industry. The large number of competing unit trusts is indicated in table 14.1, and there are at least 100 investment houses competing for the management of UK pension funds. Some aspects of competition and their impact on the allocation of investments were described in chapter 9; in the first part of this chapter some of the sources of competitiveness related to the size of insurance companies and investment houses are examined. The largest insurance company in the sample managed more than 100 times the funds managed by the smallest investment house. The negative results of statistical tests of the performance of pension funds and the size of the funds will be reported in chapter 14.

The function of fund managers is to collect and interpret information; large companies and houses have larger staffs and can collect and process more information. Some of the large companies/houses emphasised a team approach and/or a house philosophy. At other houses the pay of fund managers was geared to their performance: individual performance-related pay is not conducive to a team approach and requires a good deal of freedom for managers to select shares. There are problems of combining and using information, but the effectiveness of the systems used by the large firms to do this could not be assessed, nor could the steps they took to ensure the effectiveness with which their managers and specialists acted as teams.

Managers compete on cost and on their record. First, the sources of advantage claimed for small investment houses are outlined:

(a) Performance records and expertise are associated at least in part with individual managers and a small owner-managed house may be able to convince trustees that the managers will stay with the firm;

(b) A manager of a small fund has greater freedom to trade shares without moving the market;

(c) The performance of a relatively small fund can be influenced by the inclusion of shares of a limited number of companies with smaller capitalisations. (However, if even a small fund is invested in the

shares of small companies it will move the market against itself when
it trades these shares.)

As noted earlier, decisions on asset allocation are usually taken by a
very small number of managers at all the companies, so smaller houses
may .ot be at much disadvantage when deciding asset allocation. The
largest insurance companies can spread the cost of specialist staff: for
example, two large companies employed economists to provide assessments of economic trends and forecasts and so these companies were
not limited to using information which would be available to all
investment houses from banks and brokers. However, there can be
disadvantages in having an in-house economist filtering economic
information: a company may place undue weight on the views of its
economist. Some large insurance companies do not employ an economist to make forecasts. They believe the conventional forecast is 'in the
market' and have no reason to believe that any economist they might
employ could improve on that forecast.

Examples of cost reducing strategies for smaller investment houses
are:

(a)   to invest overseas via investment and unit trusts to avoid the cost of
       monitoring these markets and selecting shares;[1]
(b)   to have fewer shares in its portfolio, thus reducing the costs of
       managing the portfolio. (A large insurance life fund may hold 300
       shares while some funds have 30–40 shares, but one insurance
       company had only 20 shares in its managed pension fund);
(c)   by ignoring the new financial instruments – futures and traded
       options. (A house may simply ignore these instruments or use them
       only exceptionally or sparingly. A house managing large funds can
       have a team to study the futures and options markets and write futures
       and options as well as using these markets when this is assessed to be
       the most efficient way to operate in the market. Between the extreme
       approaches, houses use the new financial instruments without having
       a specialist team or having just one or two specialists. The costs of
       using the new instruments are not necessarily limited to the direct
       costs. To meet regulatory requirements, firms using the instruments
       intensively have to have computer systems which can cost £0.5m to
       put in place for monitoring price movements and positions);[2]
(d)   to rely on the analyses made by stockholders and not employ any
       analysts.

The difficulty large funds face in dealing in shares has been noted. The
introduction of new financial instruments provides large funds with
flexibility for allocating investments. For example, instead of selling
equities an investor can enter into a futures contract to sell based on
movements of the FT–SE Index but, in aggregate, dealing in futures and
options is a zero sum game for the large institutions and dealing houses

taken together because they are the principal participants in the market. So futures and options do not provide a general source of advantage for large institutions relative to smaller ones, though certain players may gain from their operations in the futures and options markets.

Strategies and approaches

There was a diversity of strategies and approaches to investment adopted by the managers interviewed. One contrast was between 'aggressive' asset management and a more conservative approach. One of the smaller insurance companies and one of the independent investment houses had aggressive policies for changing the allocation of funds between categories of investments, particularly moving in and out of equities and for trading individual shares. Transaction costs are little hindrance for aggressive funds: the managers of such funds *expect* appreciation of at least 15% relative to the market from new acquisitions, so transaction costs of 1 or 2% are not a barrier. (Trading shares of smaller companies involves higher charges than this; see p. 125). In practice, they do not always get the 15% appreciation relative to the market but, of course, they do not know in advance which shares will fail to outperform the market. Another reason for ignoring the costs is that managers know that many of their competitors pay similar charges.

Other examples of distinctive strategies were:

(a) one pension fund concentrated on high quality equities and properties; it avoided other shares and property away from prestigious locations in London. Quality properties are easier to pinpoint than quality shares; properties in Mayfair, Oxford Street, St James's and Lombard Street qualify as quality properties since the advantages of their location are unlikely to be substantially eroded. Shell, with its strong position in the oil market, BTR, because of its perceived management record and philosophy, and Reuters, because of its position in news and financial information services (a rapidly growing sector), were counted quality shares. Initial rents and dividend yields for such quality investments are likely to be relatively low;

(b) the other pension fund explicitly focused on the long term – its managers expected to be assessed over a five-year period;

(c) an insurance company which had an aggressive approach to asset allocation limited the number of shares in its managed pension fund to 20. If it liked a share it could put up to 8% of its fund into the share, and it would not hold any shares it did not expect to be able to sell within a couple of days;

(d) The investment managers of two insurance companies claimed a good record in macroeconomic forecasting. They had followed the forecasting records of the forecasters and had been able to recognise or pick the accurate forecasts. While many other houses had accepted the consensus forecast of inflation in 1988, one of the managers had acted successfully on the pessimistic forecasts:

(e)   one of the 'boutiques' which managed parts of pension funds, particularly American pension funds, also claimed expertise in assessing economic developments and interpreting their impact for international stock markets. It had a team of four economic forecasters. The firm took large 'bets' on its assessments; it claimed to have increased its holdings of Japanese shares from zero to 20% of its equity funds in October 1990 and to be holding 20% of its equity funds in the shares of companies based in France. Generally, the firm kept the funds it managed fully invested and it invested in the leading shares in each market (the alpha stocks), so that it could switch markets easily;

(f)   one investment house had specialised in investment in smaller companies. Since 1988 it had cut its exposure to small companies and did not seem to have established an alternative area of specialisation;

(g)   the approach of one investment house was to select shares with above-average dividend yields. A second objective was to increase income over time, so it selected shares with high immediate yields (its target was for a yield at least 50% above the average) and of companies which were thought to have a prospect of increasing dividends; it switched from shares which were bought for their yield but had risen in price (thus reducing the yield). The house economised on desk research and placed greater reliance on meetings with managers of companies;

(h)   two Scottish insurance companies had a common sense approach to investment – they eschewed any particular recipe, constraint or benchmark – and had a moderate turnover of shares: between 10 and 15% a year.

A question raised by the strategies and approaches adopted by fund managers concerns the nature of the skills they exercise. Plainly an ability to assess and interpret items of news based on an understanding of economic and social structures contributes to the success of any strategy or approach. Also, flexibility to change investments is important, and this requires an absence of commitment to existing investments and the managements of companies in which the investments are made, a point made by Heather Farmbrough (1990); 'the more one got to know the management, the harder it became to sell'. Apart from these general attributes there are characteristics associated with the choice of strategy. Some managers are hostile to an aggressive approach – in part, perhaps, because they themselves would find it difficult to operate such a strategy because of the speed of response and judgement thought to be required, but also because they consider the most important skill is to be able to take major decisions for the relatively long term.

Monetary approach

Three of the managers claimed to take a monetarist view of the determination of asset prices. (They seemed to the writer to be rather defensive when describing the importance they attached to the influence of monetary aggregates.) At the time of the interviews monetary policy in the US and the UK had been tightened. Lax monetary policies during the 1980s were seen as an important explanation for rising share prices, while tighter monetary policy was expected to lead to moderate increases in share prices or price falls. The expected continuing tight monetary policy during 1990 was an important influence on the decisions on liquidity taken by these three managers. More generally, the monetary indicators were considered when assessing the prospects for each economy and market.

Stakes in companies

As noted, one investment house took sizeable stakes in companies – up to 20%. The smallest investment house had large stakes in some companies which had grown rapidly by acquisition. Most insurance companies and investment houses avoided this. One reason for avoiding large stakes was to avoid being locked into a company. If a large stake is sold in the market the price is likely to fall, especially if the existence of the stake and the intention to sell are known in the market. Another reason for avoiding large stakes is that if a company or house gets involved in managing companies this activity is time consuming. A manager of a Scottish insurance company gave the example of a local company. A group of financial institutions decided the management would have to be changed, and a fund manager took two weeks sorting out the problem – during which time he was diverted from other tasks. In-house pension funds are managed by a few managers and it is said to be difficult/inefficient to use their time to monitor and influence managers of the companies in which they invest.[3] Also, fund management is a competitive industry and it is difficult to get agreement among competing fund managers on the changes required at companies in which they invest. More important, the investment houses do not have the expertise to run companies. They can suggest to managers that they reconsider certain aspects of their business or, if appropriate, that they are highly geared, but they do not have the knowledge required to advise on which R&D projects to select, or how much to spend on R&D, marketing and training.

Conclusions to part III

Although fund managers adhere to some conventions, use benchmarks and are constrained by rules imposed by actuaries and trustees, they do have flexibility in the sense that, if they expected the price of a particular company's shares to outperform the market, they would buy that share. Also, they have some scope for changing the balance of their portfolios – asset allocation – and they use it, but many managers do not stray far from the average asset allocation. Managers face keen competition, are constantly searching for ways to improve the returns on their portfolios, and individually they do not act in a perverse way.

Part IV
Other evidence

---

13 Keynes as an investor

Keynes's activities as an investor and speculator have been described in *The Collected Writings of John Maynard Keynes*, Vol. XII, pages 1–647. The following comments are based upon the material published in *The Collected Writings* and a perusal of correspondence and papers kindly made available by the National Mutual Life Assurance Society of which Keynes was Chairman from 1921 to 1938. The chronology of the material available is uneven over Keynes's career as an investor, but, fortunately, it is concentrated during the period 1937–8, the period following the publication of *The General Theory*, when as a result of illness Keynes could not attend meetings of the insurance companies of which he was a director. The material in *The Collected Writings* and held by the National Mutual Life Assurance Society consists of letters and memoranda written by Keynes and his colleagues. It is of a different quality to that of the sources used for chapter 1; naturally, Keynes would have limited objectives when writing to associates, and these writings would not necessarily represent his deeply considered views.

The purpose of this chapter is to assess the extent to which Keynes applied his theoretical description of the market in his practice as an investor. There is one piece of evidence in the correspondence that Keynes did consider that chapter 12 of *The General Theory* provided practical guidance on investment, and that he did not see it as a simple polemic: in a letter, Keynes suggested that G. H. Recknell, the actuary of the National Mutual Life Assurance Society, should read the chapter. Unfortunately, there is no further reference to the matter in the correspondence.

Keynes's successes and set-backs as an investor are described in *The Collected Writings* and are not repeated here. One clearly discernible characteristic of Keynes's investment record was that he was 'an extremely active investor. Within most of the years between 1923 and 1940, the value of the securities Keynes sold exceeded the market value of the securities he held at the beginning of the year' (the editor of *The Collected Writings*, CW, XII, p. 9). Such activity is, of course, incompatible with acceptance of the EMH.

The beauty contest

The parable of the beauty contest is the climax, though not the most important element of the analysis, of chapter 12 of *The General Theory*. There is not much evidence in the correspondence that Keynes attempted to enter such a contest as an investor; in the letters he does not spend much time attempting to foresee changes in the investment mood and the intentions of other investors. By the late 1930s his main strategy seems to have been to invest in companies which he considered to be really worth substantially in excess of current market values. He had become disenchanted with 'credit cycling' which 'means in practice selling market leaders on a falling market and buying them again on a rising one' (CW, XII, p. 100). Earlier he had related credit cycling to changes in interest rates and relative prices (CW, XII, p. 33). However, there are traces of the beauty contest approach:

> The introduction of a tariff, a change of Government, and all sorts of things quite unpredictable in advance will suddenly cause people to turn right round, to appreciate how very cheap almost everything is, and to discover that the market is completely sold out. (A memorandum written in 1931. CW, XII, p. 18)

> My feeling is that, for some little time, the errors the market will make will be definitely of pessimism and that prices will often be lower than the underlying situation really warrants rather than higher. (From a letter written in 1927. CW, XII, p. 26)

> The refusal of American investment trusts to pick up bargains as long as they believe that it is still broadly speaking a bear market is typical of credit cycling mentality. (CW, XII, p. 101)

These quotations show Keynes attempting to foresee shifts in investor sentiment. In a post-mortem written in 1938, he concluded that successful credit cycling 'needs phenomenal skill'. Also, Keynes reports that he had 'not seen a single case of success having been made out of [credit cycling]' (CW, XII, p. 100). It could be that he attached less importance to the credit cycling *and* to the beauty contest parable by 1938 than he had in 1935 when *The General Theory* was written. Although it appears that Keynes did not spend much time anticipating changes in the investment behaviour of other investors (and analysing conventions or changes in conventions which other investors adopted) he may, of course, have believed that other professional investors did so. However, there is no evidence in the correspondence that the professional investors with whom Keynes corresponded adopted the beauty contest parable either. So far, credit cycling and the parable of the beauty contest have been treated in tandem, but Keynes distinguished them. Clearly both involve short-term buying and selling; the difference is that Keynes related credit cycling to economic changes while the beauty contest parable relates it to guessing what other investors will do.

Intrinsic or fundamental values

The first quotation given above ('The introduction of a tariff ... ') demonstrates that Keynes *did* take views on the intrinsic value or real worth of assets. Examples of other occasions when he did this are:

> My purpose is to buy securities where I am satisfied as to assets and ultimate earning power and where the market price seems cheap. (CW, XII, p. 82)

> I am still convinced that one is doing a fundamentally sound thing, that is to say, backing intrinsic values, enormously in excess of market price, which at some utterly unpredictable date will in due course bring the ship home. (CW, XII, p. 77)

> The present price [of Atlas] in relation to break-up is as favourable as in the case of any of the Investment Trusts which I follow. (Letter to Recknell from Keynes, 30 January 1938)

> I think it is a grave mistake to sell these [shares in United Dominions Trust] and I put in a strong plea for the cancellation of the outstanding order ... Having regard to the market value of the gilts plus under-writing profit in respect of past years not brought to Profit and Loss, I think that you are paying extremely little for the Goodwill. The earnings yield is magnificent for a share of this class ... (Letter to Recknell from Keynes, 29 May 1937)

It is clear that Keynes did not consider that uncertainty about such matters as the price of copper, the interest rate 20 years hence, etc. prevented him taking a view on the value of the shares of some companies relative to the prices of at least some other shares and in absolute terms (see Chapter 1). In spite of uncertainty, Keynes believed he could assess what some shares were really worth. There is evidence (see below) that he was unable to assess the value of shares of other companies because he did not have sufficient information about them, and it is possible that he considered that the value of the shares of some companies could not be assessed because of uncertainty about their prospects.

Although Keynes did not foresee the timing and depth of the recessions at the beginning of the 1930s and in 1937, he did take a view on likely economic changes and their impact on the market.

... if and when there is a genuine recovery in America, this combined with the level of armament expenditure is capable of making 1939 quite a good year [for shares]. (CW, XII, p. 43)

Optimistic stance

The 1931 quotation about unpredictable future events leading people to realise how cheap shares were (given on p. 136) suggests Keynes took an optimistic view of future developments at that time. An example of optimism which was not vindicated in the event was:

I think your conclusions are too bearish ... Further, the result of reflection is to make me think it is unlikely that there will be any serious set back of general trade (as distinct from special lines) for any appreciable period. The force of cheaper money will soon predominate over other adverse influences. (Letter to Recknell from Keynes, 16 November 1929)

Another example of Keynes's optimism proving unjustified was that he was heavily invested at the end of 1936 and was hit hard by the falls in security prices in 1937. At the end of 1936 he had expected the recovery in America to continue and did not foresee the recession that occurred. The important point is not that he failed to foresee the recession, but that his decisions at this time were consistent for someone who generally took an optimistic view of the future.

Concentration of investments

When an investor looks back, an inevitable question is: 'Why didn't I put my money into the winners and less into the losers?' Of course, concentration of investment in a few shares would increase the chances of large gains and large losses. Keynes emphasised the importance of information:

I preferred one investment about which I had sufficient information to form a judgement to ten securities about which I know little or nothing. (CW, XII, p. 81)

I am quite incapable of having adequate knowledge of more than a very limited range of investments ... (CW, XII, p. 82)

Nevertheless, King's has done ... better than the Provincial. I am quite sure the reason for this is that our unit of investment ... has been so much larger. [King's College had fewer investments but on average had proportionately more committed to each investment] (CW, XII, p. 83)

In a post-mortem on investment policy written in May 1938 in the aftermath of a fall in share prices Keynes wrote:

I believe now that successful investment depends on three principles:
(1) a careful selection of a few investments (or a few types of investment) having regard to their cheapness in relation to their probable actual and potential *intrinsic* value over a period of years ahead and in relation to alternative investments at the time;

(2) a steadfast holding of these in fairly large units through thick and thin, perhaps for several years, until either they have fulfilled their promise or it is evident that they were purchased on a mistake;

(3) a *balanced* investment position, i.e. a variety of risks in spite of individual holdings being large, and if possible opposed risks (e.g. a holding of gold shares amongst other equities) since they are likely to move in opposite directions when there are general fluctuations. (CW, XII, p. 106–7)

14 The performance of fund managers

Fund managers can seek to beat the index in one of two ways: by varying the allocation of funds to classes of investment (including cash deposits), or by selecting superior stocks. The extent to which fund managers have freedom to vary the allocation of funds differs; managers of 'managed funds' have the freedom to move between a range of categories of investment, while managers of funds for investment in, say, Japan are restricted.

Unit trusts

Some commentators question why investors use and pay for professional fund managers at all; these commentators point to the fact that in the past fund managers have not on average outperformed the FT–Actuaries All Share Index, though some have done do handsomely, and others have fallen far short. They suggest investors would do better to invest directly and avoid the charges.

The investment record of unit trust fund managers for varying periods ending on 1 July, 1990 as recorded in *Money Management* for August 1990, is summarised in table 14.1.[1] The method of calculating returns on investments was described in Box 4. The basis of the performance comparisons is the return on investments using offer to bid quotations and with net income (after tax and after the annual management charges) reinvested. The offer price includes the initial charges, and the bid price is the amount the investor receives on selling his investments, so the performance records represent the net returns to investors from investments. The FT–Actuaries All Share Index with which the funds are compared in table 14.1 is adjusted to include reinvestment of notional, after tax-income, but before any adjustment for notional management charges.

Money Management separates the unit trusts into broad categories depending upon the type of specialisation of the trusts. Table 14.1

Table 14.1. *The performance of unit trusts to 1 July 1990 (£1,000 invested at the beginning of the period)*[a]

	3 years (£s)	5 years (£s)	10 years (£s)
FT–Actuaries UK All Share Index[b]	1,091	2,202	5,798
Unit trusts			
UK General			
average	1,005	2,102	5,694
top performing trust	1,175	2,727	8,161
worst performing trust	660	1,386	2,785
number of trusts outperforming the FT–Actuaries Index	12	23	27
number of trusts	88	74	55
UK Growth			
average	870	2,009	5,049
top performing trust	1,175	3,678	10,831
worst performing trust	483	1,185	1,856
number of trusts outperforming the FT–Actuaries Index	4	21	13
number of trusts	147	105	60
UK Equity Income			
average	1,017	2,277	6,062
top performing trust	1,356	3,387	9,138
worst performing trust	618	1,580	3,870
number of trusts outperforming the FT–Actuaries Index	20	44	22
number of trusts	107	79	50
Standard and Poor's (S&P) Composite Index	1,178	1,866	3,134
North America[c]			
average	1,001	1,293	3,842
top performing trust	1,401	1,888	6,001
worst performing trust	677	840	2,678
number of trusts outperforming the S&P Index	7	1	19
number of trusts	115	82	27
Insurance funds			
Managed			
average	1,048	1,634	3,110
number of funds	160	113	54
UK equity			
average	1,000	1,837	4,073
number of funds	168	139	64

Notes: [a] Net income after tax at the standard rate on dividends and management charges is reinvested.
[b] This is a hypothetical index with net after-tax income reinvested.
[c] Includes trusts investing in Canada.
Source: Money Management, August 1990.

shows that 27 out of 55 UK 'General Unit Trusts' beat the index over the period of ten years to 1 July 1990. A period of about ten years is a fair period to use to assess the performance of unit trusts, since over short periods charges are a substantial cost. (When assessing the performance of funds in terms of capital appreciation and return it is important to note that the 1980s were a very favourable period for investment in equities.) Comparing performance over a shorter period, the five years to 1 July 1990, only 23 out of 74 trusts beat the index, and over three years this was achieved by only 12 out of 88 trusts. In contrast, over both five-year and ten-year periods, the 'UK Equity Income Trusts' on average gave a slightly higher return than the FT–Actuaries All Share Index, and taking the three groups of UK unit trusts which are distinguished in Table 14.1 together, 62 out of the 165 trusts beat the index over ten years; the average underperformance over that period was less than 1% *a year* in terms of total return.

The top performing trusts in each sector beat the *increase* in the index by 49% or more, while the worst performing trusts in the first two classes, 'UK General' and 'UK Growth' ended the period with values less than 50% of the benchmark FT–Actuaries All Share Index. (One attraction of investing in unit trusts as compared to depositing money with building societies for some investors is that there is a chance of a large win; other investors are repelled by the risk of a loss.) One explanation for the differences in performance is that the categories distinguished are broad and trusts with different investment objectives and criteria are included in each class. The spectacular outperformance of the index by some unit trusts over a ten-year period and dismal underperformance by others is noteworthy for another reason – it seems to conflict with the EMH, which suggests it would be difficult to greatly outperform (or underperform) the index, at least if a trust held a broad selection of shares and did not underperform by incurring heavy transaction costs.

The performance of funds is shown in table 14.1 after deducting the charges made by managers of the funds. Taking these as an initial charge of 6% and an annual charge of 1%, and assuming the performance of the trusts is even in proportional terms over the period of ten years to 1 July 1990, then these charges would reduce the final results for a new investor by 15%. These charges represent a handicap of 15% of the final investment when comparisons are made with the FT–Actuaries All Share Index with notional net income reinvested, but with no deduction for notional charges. The performance of the unit trust funds over ten years compared to the FT–Actuaries All Share Index adjusted for these notional management charges is more impressive – 41 out of 55 'UK General' funds outperformed this index, 31 out of 60 'UK Growth' funds and 43 out of 50 'UK Equity Income' funds did so. In total, 115 out of 165 unit trusts beat the index in the sense that they outperformed the index with the funds they managed, *before deducting their charges*. But there is a significant qualification to this result: ten years earlier, in August 1980, there were 300 unit trusts in the three classifications – nearly half the funds had been amalgamated or closed, and these tended to be among the weaker performing funds prior to amalgamation or closure (see below).[2]

Insurance funds

Managed insurance fund units can invest in a range of assets, including UK and overseas equities, traditional bonds, index-linked bonds, property and deposits. A comparison between the performance of managed insurance funds, shown at the foot of table 14.1, and that of the FT–Actuaries All Share Index, which reflects the movement of UK equities and is shown at the top of the same table, is of interest. Managed funds underperformed the index during the 1980s when investment in UK equities (and overseas equities) produced higher returns than investments in bonds or deposits, as they had done in earlier post-war decades, and fund managers did not foresee these differences in performance and invest all their funds in equities.

Winners, losers and the persistence of performance

Tables 14.2 and 14.3 record the performance of winning and losing unit trusts over the ten years to July 1990. The performance of each fund measured by the percentage return over the ten years to 1 July 1990 is shown in the first row of both tables, and this is followed by the return for each of the ten years. The product of the returns for the individual years shown in the last row of the tables does not equal the return for the ten-year period because from 1985 each of the returns for individual years is calculated from the offer price at the beginning of the year to the bid price at the end of the year. With a constant spread of 6% this would result in the ten-year return being 52% higher than that for the product of the individual years. M&G Midland Trust,[3] the winner of the 'UK General' class with a percentage return of 716% over ten years (compared to the 480% shown by the FT–Actuaries All Share Index) was among the top ten trusts for five consecutive years and in only three years was it in the bottom half of the list. Henderson Income and Growth was in the top half of the list in eight out of ten years. MLA General started well, but was in the bottom half of the list in each of the final six years.

Table 14.2. Persistence of performance of the 'winners' (10 years to July 1990)[a]

1. UK General

	M&G Midland				Henderson Income and Growth[b]				MLA General			
	position	total no. of trusts	% return over year or years[c]	fund size (£m)	position	total no. of trusts	% return over year or years[c]	fund size (£m)	position	total no. of trusts	% return over year or years[c]	fund size (£m)
Over 10 years	1	55	716		2	55	695		3	55	677	
Year[d] 1	72	102	11	12.6	2	102	41	2.2	3	104	51	0.7
2	21	95	8	13.9	10	95	10	6.3	7	86	13	3.3
3	59	97	38	19.5	5	97	58	15.7	1	80	82	0.9
4	2	82	31	30.7	46	97	18	40.2	28	76	11	30.2
5	4	88	31	35.0	38	88	20	46.1	67	88	14	38.9
6	9	87	41	50.9	7	87	42	72.4	47	87	33	59.1
7	6	94	59	80.4	38	94	39	120.4	69	94	32	84.3
8	4	101	−7	109.3	35	101	−17	115.0	58	101	−19	74.2
9	12	100	16	199.3	83	100	6	101.2	61	100	9	87.2
10	88	99	−11	215.0	69	99	−4	95.3	86	99	−9	76.2
Product of single year (% increases)[e]			511				466				466	

2. UK Growth

	Fidelity Special Situations				Govett UK Small Companies				Capability Special Situations[f]			
	position	total no. of trusts	% return over year or years[b]	fund size (£m)	position	total no. of trusts	% return over year or years[c]	fund size (£m)	position	total no. of trusts	% return over year or years[c]	fund size (£m)
Over 10 years	1	60	983		2	60	927		3	60	696	
Year 1	9	96	45	4.6					68	104	21	0.6
2	61	72	−13	5.3					60	86	−2	2.4
3	5	83	87	6.8					26	83	57	3.8
4	52	97	6	10.2					19	97	14	4.8
5	21	96	22	13.3					2	96	48	23.0
6	10	117	55	11.0					16	117	52	27.6
7	52	132	58	96.0					76	132	46	25.7
8	12	151	−11	117.0	25	101	−16	9.5	63	151	−19	25.7
9	1	195	26	251.0	3	195	25	16.4	61	195	10	27.4
10	92	198	−9	317.0	111	198	−11	29.7	82	198	−6	22.4
Product of single year (% increases)[e]			662								484	

Table 14.2. (cont.)

3. UK Equity Income

	Key Income				Abbey High Income Equity				James Capel Income			
	position	total no. of trusts	% return over year or years[c]	fund size (£m)	position	total no. of trusts	% return over year or years[c]	fund size (£m)	position	total no. of trusts	% return over year or years[c]	fund size (£m)
Over 10 years	1	50	814		2	50	732		3	50	703	
Year 1	61	102	13	0.4	59	102	14	1.4	35	102	19	2.3
2	6	94	12	0.4	56	94	3	3.6	2	94	15	3.0
3	47	97	41	0.4	62	97	37	9.5	53	97	40	4.2
4	4	82	28	0.7	18	82	23	22.3	9	82	26	6.3
5	11	80	26	1.4	68	80	13	25.0	4	80	30	6.7
6	36	95	48	2.7	53	95	36	43.0	15	95	45	12.6
7	1	110	68	5.6	52	110	41	55.6	93	110	33	16.8
8	2	120	1	22.0	82	120	−15	71.2	68	120	−14	17.0
9	75	118	6	54.9	33	118	10	84.5	37	118	10	20.2
10	112	123	−13	39.7	23	123	0	82.2	6	123	4	27.0
Product of single year (% increases)[e]			567				301				495	

4. North America

	Fidelity American				M&G American & Gen. Accident				M&G American Recovery			
	position	total no. of trusts	% return over year or years[b]	fund size (£m)	position	total no. of trusts	% return over year or years[c]	fund size (£m)	position	total no. of trusts	% return over year or years[c]	fund size (£m)
Over 10 years	1	27	500		2	27	468		3	27	453	
Year 1	5	34	88	7.3	18	34	57	63.4	7	34	84	18.2
2	18	39	−12	18.7	4	39	−6	88.3	6	39	−7	38.5
3	12	46	212	32.0	30	46	91	112.0	4	46	226	60.7
4	31	54	−15	33.9	1	54	3	130.5	25	54	−11	62.5
5	32	177	19	35.2	2	77	36	143.1	16	77	25	66.7
6	26	89	17	46.0	49	89	11	205.4	58	89	9	85.1
7	14	99	11	95.1	58	99	2	210.8	72	99	−1	78.0
8	42	115	−21	76.0	32	115	−19	147.6	14	115	−15	52.9
9	5	122	30	148.0	26	122	24	185.7	30	122	23	77.4
10	56	123	−5	187.0	56	123	−5	201.6	116	123	−16	70.2
Product of single year (% increases)[e]			562				327				488	

Notes: [a] The underlining of fund size indicates a break in the series. [b] Years 1 to 4 included in 'UK Equity Income' class. [c] The returns are based on the change from the offer price at the beginning of the period to the bid price at the end of the period for the ten-year comparison and for years 5 to 10, but for years 1 to 4 the returns are based on comparisons of the offer price at the beginning of the period to offer price at the end. [d] Year 1 is 1980/1, Year 2 is 1981/2, etc.
[e] $\left(\dfrac{(100 + \% \,\text{Yr1})}{100} \cdot \dfrac{(100 + \% \,\text{Yr2})}{100} \cdots \dfrac{(100 + \% \,\text{Yr10})}{100} \right) - 100$
[f] Years 1 and 2 named the 'Alben Trust'; years 3 to 8 titled 'Vanguard Special Situations'.
Sources: Money Management, August each year, 1981–1990. Unit Trust Yearbook, 1981–1990.

Table 14.3. *Persistence of performance of the 'losers' (10 years to July 1990)*

1. UK General

	Asset Growth[a]				Discretionary				Buckmaster General[b]			
	position	total no. of trusts	% return over year or years[a]	fund size (£m)	position	total no. of trusts	% return over year or years[c]	fund size (£m)	position	total no. of trusts	% return over year or years[c]	fund size (£m)
Over 10 years	55	55	<u>179</u>	-	54	55	<u>217</u>	6.5	53	55	<u>317</u>	3.0
Year 1	91	104	14	0.3	36	104	27	8.0	63	104	22	3.1
2	3	86	17		15	86	9	<u>9.1</u>	84	86	-18	<u>3.8</u>
3	78	80	26	0.4	79	80	26	9.1	10	80	60	3.5
4	41	76	8	0.8	60	76	5	9.6	70	76	2	4.4
5	88	88	-3	0.8	86	88	4	11.0	27	88	22	5.6
6	87	87	14	3.5	26	87	32	10.6	51	87	33	8.3
7	14	94	46	4.3	23	94	44	13.8	11	94	49	7.7
8	88	101	-23	3.1	1	101	0	13.8	91	101	-24	9.1
9	95	100	4		28	100	13	13.0	9	100	17	8.8
10	97	99	-19	-	99	99	-23		82	99	-7	
Product of single year (% increases)[d]			90				212				226	

2. UK Growth

	Robert Fraser Growth[e]				Brown Shipley Recovery				Allied Dunbar 2nd Small Cos.[f]			
	position	total no. of trusts	% return over year or years[c]	fund size (£m)	position	total no. of trusts	% return over year or years[c]	fund size (£m)	position	total no. of trusts	% return over year or years[c]	fund size (£m)
Over 10 years	60	60	86	0.2	59	60	155	0.3	58	60	198	14.8
Year 1	97	104	9		90	96	11	0.3	25	96	35	20.7
2	86	86	−24		71	72	−26		11	172	5	
3	80	80	8	0.2	69	83	36	0.5	57	83	44	31.5
4	76	76	−16	0.2	10	97	20	0.5	55	97	6	33.3
5	25	88	22	0.2	72	96	8	0.8	79	96	5	34.6
6	23	87	37	0.9	7	117	61	2.2	103	117	22	34.7
7	2	94	69	2.3	6	132	84	4.0	26	132	68	37.8
8	90	101	−24	3.5	114	151	−24	24.2	144	151	−33	25.1
9	98	100	2	2.1	191	195	6	16.6	184	195	−3	22.1
10	170	198	−20	1.4	197	198	−40	5.4	186	198	−28	12.0
Product of single year (% increases)[d]			32				84				118	

Table 14.3. (cont.)

3. UK Equity Income	Guinness Mahon St. Vincent High Income[g]				Guinness Mahon High Income[h]				Wardley Income[i]			
	position	total no. of trusts	% return over year or years[c]	fund size (£m)	position	total no. of trusts	% return over year or years[c]	fund size (£m)	position	total no. of trusts	% return over year or years[c]	fund size (£m)
Over 10 years	50	50	287		49	50	334		48	50	347	
Year 1	74	102	10		62	102	5	0.6	78	102	9	1.0
2	81	94	−2		74	94	0	0.5	86	94	−5	1.0
3	92	97	24		95	97	18	0.5	94	97	22	1.0
4	74	82	10	1.7	61	82	15	0.5	22	82	22	3.0
5	56	80	15	2.0	78	80	−1	0.5	1	16	12	4.6
6	79	95	32	2.8	76	95	33	0.6	3	19	43	5.6
7	44	110	44	3.4	28	110	48	0.6	3	19	51	6.7
8	23	120	−10	3.3	1	120	13	12.6	8	23	−12	10.6
9	29	118	10	4.6	100	118	4	30.2	77	118	6	13.2
10	40	123	−2	4.6	87	123	−7	16.8	70	123	−5	9.4
Product of single year (% increases)[d]			212				309				230	

4. North America

	Target American Eagle				Guinness Mahon N. America[j]				Wardley American[k]			
	position	total no. of trusts	% return over year or years[c]	fund size (£m)	position	total no. of trusts	% return over year or years[c]	fund size (£m)	position	total no. of trusts	% return over year or years[c]	fund size (£m)
Over 10 years	27	27	168		26	27	171	0.5	25	27	175	2.0
Year 1	22	34	55		21	34	55	0.4	34	34	29	3.4
2	27	39	-18		33	39	-20	0.4	19	39	-12	4.7
3	14	46	111		46	46	54	0.3	25	46	95	4.3
4	48	54	-22	9.0	6	54	-2	0.3	7	54	-3	4.3
5	69	77	4	12.1	38	77	18	0.3	55	77	12	6.7
6	76	89	5	16.2	79	89	0	0.3	77	89	1	7.0
7	65	99	1	12.2	53	99	3	0.3	32	99	8	7.1
8	39	115	-20	8.2	41	115	-20	0.1	108	115	-30	3.3
9	97	122	5	10.2	15	122	25	1.7	43	122	21	5.1
10	81	123	-8	8.1	98	123	-11	8.1	99	123	-11	5.2
Product of single year (% increases)[d]			78				102				98	

[a] Years 1 to 4 named 'College Hill'; years 5 to 6 titled 'Heritable Growth'.   [b] Years 1 to 3 titled 'Buckingham'.
[c] See Table 14.2, note c.   [d] See Table 14.2, note e.   [e] Years 1 to 9 under 'UK General'.
[f] Years 1 to 4 named 'Allied Hambro 2nd Small Cos.'.
[g] Years 1 to 3 named 'Craigmount Midmount'; Years 4 to 8 titled 'St. Vincent High Income'.
[h] Years 1 to 3 listed as 'Craigmount High Income'; Years 4 to 5 titled 'Temple Bar High Income'.
[i] Year 1 named 'Gibbs Income'; Years 2 to 3 as 'HK Income'; Years 5 to 8 under title of 'UK Mixed Income'.
[j] Years 1 to 3 listed as 'Craigmount North American'; Years 4 to 5 as Temple Bar American.
[k] Year 1 named 'Gibbs American'; Years 2–3 listed as 'HK American'.   Sources: As for Table 14.2.

In the 'UK Growth' category, Fidelity Special Situations was among the top ten trusts in five years and in only two years was it in the bottom half of the list. In spite of the greatly increased size of the trust towards the end of the period, it was first in the penultimate year.

Three M&G trusts are included among the twelve winners so this company's investment strategy is of particular interest:

M&G's investment philosophy is to concentrate on long-term value with an emphasis on income and recovery and a general reluctance to invest in highly rated fashionable stocks ... as substantial shareholders we should have a firm and lasting relationship with managements of companies in which we have a large interest ... we find that constructive intervention can often be preferable to disposing of a holding. (*M&G Yearbook*, 1990)

Although M&G's trusts have an impressive record they are not among the winning trusts every year.

The records of the losers shown in table 14.3 are the reverse of those for the winners. In the 'UK General' class, Asset Growth had the worst record and was in the bottom half in eight out of ten years and among the bottom three no less than four times. A feature of the comparisons is that the worst performers end the period much smaller in terms of funds managed than the winners.

As many of the best and worst performing trusts are small, at least at the beginning of the period, the performance of the largest trusts at the end of July 1981 was examined and the results are shown in table 14.4. The worst performing large UK trust showed a return of 390% over ten years compared to the notional return for the FT–Actuaries All Share Index of 480%, while the best performing large trust was M&G Dividend with a return of 611%: the results are within ±30% of the return shown by the FT–Actuaries All Share Index. (It is notable that the size of six of the twelve trusts listed in table 14.4 increased, but by much less than the return over the ten years – funds were withdrawn from these trusts.)

The American term for unit trusts is mutual funds: a recent study of the performance of US mutual funds over the period 1976–1988 suggests that above and below average performance persists. 'A superior return for a given mutual fund over a two year horizon increases the probability that the fund will have a superior return in the following two year period' (Goetzmann and Ibbotson, 1990).

Performance and changes in size of funds

The relationship between the performance of trusts and changes in their size was examined for a five-year period and then on an annual basis. Performance affects the size of unit trusts in two ways – increases

Table 14.4. *The performance of the largest funds (measured at 31 July 1991)*

Class and fund	Fund size £(m) 1981	Fund size £(m) 1990	Percentage return over 10 years	Position in class in 1991	Number of funds in class
UK General					
S&P Investment Trust[a]	215	344	438	4	5
TSB General	110	615	399	41	55
M&G General	99	333	515	18	55
UK Growth					
Barclays Unicorn Capital	62	101	414	27	60
M&G Recovery	51	699	545	10	60
Allied Hambro Accumulator[b]	47	703	390	43	55
UK Equity Income					
M&G Dividend	98	608	611	9	50
Barclays Unicorn Income	60	317	531	17	50
S&P High Yield	50	121	508	22	50
North American					
M&G American & General	54	202	468	2	27
Hill Samuel Dollar	48	44	334	16	27
S&P US Growth	41	104	374	6	27

Notes: [a] In 1990 the trust was classified as 'Investment Trust Units' not 'UK General'.
[b] Name changed to 'Allied Dunbar Accumulator' in 1985 and moved to 'UK General' class in 1988.
Sources: Money Management, August 1981 and August 1990; *Unit Trust Yearbook,* 1981.

in the price of units directly increase funds under management, and a relatively good performance attracts new investment. Table 14.5 shows the number of unit trusts surviving over a period of six years, 1985 to 1991, and the changes in the size of funds over this period. For this analysis the ten best performing unit trusts and the ten worst performing unit trusts over the period 1 July 1980 to 1 July 1985 were selected and their progress over the following six years compared. Some were merged with, or their units transferred to, other trusts. The change in the fund size was calculated for those that did not undergo mergers or

Table 14.5. Performance of unit trusts, 1980–5 and changes in size, 1985–91[a]

		Type of unit trust								
		UK General		UK Growth		UK Equity Income		North American		All types
		best 10	worst 10	best 10	worst 10	best 10	worst 10	best 10	worst 10	best 40	worst 40
Number of unit trusts merging or transferring	1986	0	0	0	3	0	5	0	4	0	12
	1987	0	2	1	1	1	1	0	2	2	6
	1988	0	0	1	1	1	0	0	1	2	2
	1989	0	0	0	0	0	2	0	1	0	3
	1990	0	1	1	0	0	0	0	0	1	1
	1991	0	0	0	1	0	0	1	0	1	1
No. of unit trusts surviving to end of period		10	7	7	4	8	2	9	2	34	15
Percentage change in fund size[b]	1986	+58	+17	+23	+18	+77	+31	+22	+10	+43	+17
	1987	+45	+43	+117	+27	+41	+30	+3	−4	+35	+26
	1988	+6	+3	+34	+27	+0	+9	−25	−31	+0	+4
	1989	+42	+1	+23	−12	+17	+57	+14	+22	+27	+0
	1990	−23	−11	+6	−14	−3	+117	+15	+13	−8	−17
	1991	+2	+16	−11	−14	+2	−42	−9	+9	−2	+15
	1986–91	+175	+78	+392	+64	+195	+386	+14	−33	+134	+27

[a] All years to 1 July.   [b] The percentage change in the total funds managed by the surviving trusts.
Source: *Money Management*, and *The Unit Trust Year Book*, various years.

Table 14.6. *Performance of unit trusts and changes in size the following year*

Type of unit trust	Years to 1 July				
	1986	1987	1988	1989	1990
All types of unit trust included in the analysis					
Number survived from best 20	19	20	19	18	20
Number survived from worst 20	17	18	12	18	18
Percentage change in fund size: best 20[a]	+77	+11	+42	+18	+23
Percentage change in fund size: worst 20[a]	+38	−8	+1	+6	−7
General (UK) unit trusts					
Number survived from best 5	5	5	5	5	5
Number survived from worst 5	4	5	4	5	5
Percentage change in fund size: best 5[a]	+69	+190	+54	+8	+33
Percentage change in fund size: worst 5[a]	+43	−1	+4	+64	−5
UK growth unit trusts pension funds					
Number survived from best 5	5	5	5	4	5
Number survived from worst 5	5	4	3	4	4
Percentage change in fund size: best 5[a]	+103	−32	−10	+26	+30
Percentage change in fund size: worst 5[a]	+115	−3	−18	−59	−68
UK equity income unit trusts					
Number survived from best 5	5	5	4	4	5
Number survived from worst 5	4	4	1	4	4
Percentage change in fund size: best 5[a]	+70	+68	+118	+10	+21
Percentage change in fund size: worst 5[a]	+25	+412	+72	−18	−7
North American unit trusts					
Number survived from best 5	4	5	5	5	5
Number survived from worst 5	4	5	4	5	5
Percentage change in fund size: best 5[a]	+170	−18	+14	+34	+4
Percentage change in fund size: worst 5[a]	−2	−55	+14	−18	+99

Note: [a] The percentage change in the total funds managed at the end of the year.
Sources: *Money Management*, August 1985–91. *The Unit Trust Year Book*, Autumn 1990.

transfers for each year and over the entire period (unit trusts which only underwent name changes were retained in the analysis). This process was then repeated for the ten worst performing unit trusts.

A problem for comparing changes in the size of funds in later years and over the 1985 to 1991 period as a whole was the shortage of observations. By 1991, only two of the ten worst performing UK Equity Income unit trusts between 1980 and 1985 had survived. These might be regarded as the best of the worst, and this could explain the 386% rise in the fund size. But the management of the trusts may also have changed. Over the three years when only these two out of the initial ten unit trusts existed – 1989 to 1991 – they outperformed the best performing UK Equity Income unit trusts.

The results of the second test of the link between performance and changes in size of trusts are shown in table 14.6. The changes in size of the best performing unit trusts in each of the four categories each year (to 1 July) during the following year were compared. Again, some trusts merged with or transferred their units to other unit trusts and so did not 'survive' the year. For those that survived, the change in the aggregate of the funds was calculated. (Again, any name changes in unit trusts were ignored.) The process was repeated for each year between 1986 and 1990 and for the worst five in each year and category.

The best performing trusts have a higher survival rate and so any assessment of the *overall* performance of unit trusts has to include trusts which drop out. Also, there is a clear pattern of the best performing trusts increasing in size faster than the worst performing trusts.

Pension funds

The WM Company analyses and compares the investment performance of pension funds. Performance is calculated before *deducting* management charges because the WM Company compares 'the managers' stock market performance not their skill at negotiating fees'. In their report for 1989 they commented, 'the evidence of the past decade shows that neither asset allocation decisions, nor stock selection have contributed strongly to the returns of pension funds over a passive investment simulation'. The funds would have achieved a better average performance if they had all invested in the Index. However, the underperformance was slight: for all equities held by the funds surveyed by the WM Company the annual return averaged 0.6% a year less than for the FT–Actuaries All Share Index between 1979 and 1989. The comparisons made by the Combined Actuarial Performance Services Ltd (CAPS) show a median return on UK equities for the 1,524

UK pension funds it compared of 23.8% per year between 1980 and 1989, compared to the Index return of 23.6%. The upper quartile return was 24.7% and the lower quartile 23%. Over the same period the median return for the pension funds' total investments, including property, was much lower, 19.6% per year; the upper quartile return was 20.3%, the lower quartile 18.9%, the first decile was 21.1% and the ninth decile 18.1% per year. These comparisons indicate that the investment performance of pension funds is (as would be expected because their investment objectives are more homogeneous) less dispersed than for unit trusts.

Turnover

The WM Company also records turnover of shares by pension funds; it defines turnover activity as:

$$\frac{\text{purchases} + \text{sales} - \text{investment}}{\text{mean fund}}$$

In 1989 turnover activity averaged 77% of the capitalisation of UK equity investments. In effect, the funds sold and bought UK shares to a value of nearly 40% of their holdings. The average turnover activity for UK equities held by the funds during the four years 1986 to 1989 was 68%. For overseas equities it averaged 122% – in effect, the funds changed more than half their overseas portfolios each year. The WM Company comment that an analysis they made 'indicates no correlation between activity and return ... the effect of higher dealing costs (with higher activity) is compensated by higher returns, but there is no overall gain'. CAPS (1990) states that for the funds it compared there was a negative correlation between UK equity performance and activity in 1989 but that the correlation was positive in 1987 and not significant in all other years.

The WM Company (1990, p. 14) provides estimates of dealing costs; for UK equities its estimates are 0.7% for purchases and 0.2% for sales in 1989. A sale and a purchase cost approximately 1%. The jobbers' turn depends on the size of a company and trading in its shares; for shares of a few leading companies, such as BT, the turn is less than 0.5%, but for companies outside the leading 100, the jobbers' turn is higher, rising to 2% for medium-sized companies and as much as 10% for small ones whose shares are traded infrequently. Also, dealing costs for overseas stocks are higher – 0.6% for purchases and 0.8% for sales, according to the WM Company. Estimates obtained from the investment managers of trusts put costs for dealing in overseas shares even higher – a switch out of leading Japanese shares to leading German shares could, with the jobbers' turn, cost 3%. Assuming the average dealing costs are 1.5% for a combined sale and purchase, if 40% of a fund were turned over during a year, dealing costs would be 0.6% of the capitalisation of the fund – in line with the underperformance of the funds monitored by the WM Company.

Other results

An important result of the comparisons of performance made by the WM Company is that differences in performance are primarily attributable to share selection rather than to allocation between different classes of securities or the timing of investment decisions. From an examination of the performance of the top and bottom quartiles of pension funds ranked by performance, the WM Company concludes that 'selection ... dominates the factors which differentiate top and bottom performance'. This conclusion contrasts with the view of fund managers reported at the beginning of chapter 10 who placed market allocation ahead of share selection as a determinant of performance.

CAPS (1990) reports the results of statistical tests of the relationship between performance and the size of funds. Evidence of a positive correlation was found for the 1988 results, but that 'there has been no persistent relationship between performance and size of funds'.

The fees charged for managing pension fund investments usually include a performance element. Fees which exclude dealing costs range from a minimum of about 0.3% for managing equities or mixed funds with discretion to select shares and allocate investments to sectors, to 2.5% of the fund for outstanding performance relative to a particular index. These fees have to be subtracted from the returns reported earlier. Fees for managing tracker funds (funds which track an index by distributing the investments of the fund in line with the weighting of shares used for the index which is tracked) or gilts are lower. One large insurance company was reported to have won a contract to manage a part of a pension fund on a tracker basis for a fee of less than 0.1% of the value of the fund per year. For equity funds, fees are thought to average about 0.75% a year, but there is uncertainty about this estimate. Consulting actuaries suggested the average figure reported here; however, some fund managers considered the figure was high.

General

In this study, the investment managers who were interviewed are referred to as professional investors, implying they are 'investors possessing judgement and knowledge beyond that of the average private investor'. The fact that, on average, the funds managed by professional investors after deducting transaction costs and their charges, underperform the indices portraying the movement of the market as a whole is not surprising. Collectively, institutions will underperform these indices unless they can win at the expense of private or overseas-based investors in UK equities. As the holdings of private and overseas-based investors are relatively small and some private investors have inside knowledge or access to better information, the scope for winning is limited.[4]

There are two alternatives to using professional fund managers – doing the job oneself or selecting investments randomly (or with the proverbial pin). If investors do the job themselves, they might decide to make very few switches as a matter of principle so that the job of managing investments virtually disappears. An investor who adopts this strategy should diversify his or her investments (within limits) and should usually try to avoid investing in companies which are in fashion – shares whose prices have recently risen rapidly and/or which have low yields. In spite of their generally mediocre average performance in the past, fund managers might be expected to make better judgements in the future than average private individuals or a pin; the future may be different from the past: for example, in the future the return on fixed interest investments might exceed that on equities for a period, if the government really does sustain a policy of giving priority to reducing inflation to below, say, 3% a year whatever the consequences for unemployment. Investment managers of funds with freedom to switch investments may consider and assess such possibilities, a strategy which would not occur to some private investors. The danger is, of course, that the investor selects a fund managed by a manager who goes on a succession of wild goose chases incurring heavy transaction costs, whether or not he also anticipates any significant long-term changes in returns for different classes of investment.

In conclusion, the comparisons of the performance of unit trusts show a wide range of performance, with some funds outperforming the indices over long periods.

15 The Press

The extensive coverage of City news indicates that the newspapers are an important source of information and comment upon the stock market, at least for private as opposed to institutional investors. Some City editors seem to believe they can predict movements of share prices for their readers, but before reviewing their advice, I should like to report a prediction made by William Rees Mogg in *The Independent* on 27 October 1987, following the crash. (Rees Mogg is a former editor of *The Times* and a director of the investment house M&G.) This prediction is unusual because it takes a view of the market three years ahead:

> If one fits the pattern [of the 1929 crash] to 1987, it would suggest that world stock markets will be in shock until late November, will have a substantial recovery until the beginning of May 1988, but will then go into profound decline which will not reach its bottom until the middle of 1990.
>
> The investment advice is simple. Do not sell now. Sell equities early next year in a spring rally. Buy high grade bonds with the proceeds. Hold them for two years.

(In fact between March 1988 and March 1990 equities *rose* by 22% and *bonds* fell by 21%. The gross interest yield on bonds would have been approximately 8% higher than the dividend yield on equities over the two-year period).

The quotation is interesting for several reasons. Plainly, Rees Mogg's forecasts were wrong, but in one sense his diagnosis of the position was perceptive; he pinpointed the fact that the effect of deregulation of the world financial system had been to lead to an explosion of credit and unsound lending, and that this had weakened the financial position of banks and would lead to crisis. However, his assessment of the situation was far too apocalyptic; so far, at least, governments have been able to forestall a major crisis.

Most of the comment in the City columns of the Press about the stock market focuses on a much shorter time horizon than Rees Mogg's comment. Examples of the very diverse comments are:

There is a more bearish feel about the UK equity market than there was a fortnight ago. (*Financial Times*, 'Lex', 7 March 1990)

The market's low valuation and the institutions' cash piles argue that investors should, at the least, have little to lose by moving in now. (*Investors Chronicle*, 'Market View', 21 December 1989)

The question is whether the latest ERM rally is a fundamental change of direction or a mere interlude in a bear market. If anything, yesterday's evidence points to the latter. (*Financial Times*, 'Lex', 9 October 1990)

If we do have a war, shares will fall sharply, then rally, as the institutions try to take advantage of the lower prices, but this will not last and prices will fall again at least to the 1800 level and probably below that. (*Sunday Times*, 13 January 1991)

The nature and accuracy of Press comment about future movements of share prices was examined first for 1990, a year in which the FT–Actuaries 500 Share Index fell by 11%. Five sources were surveyed including three Sunday newspapers – readers may have more time to study comment in the Sunday Press. The comments made in the 'Lex' column of the *Financial Times*, 'Market View' in the *Investors Chronicle*, the 'Viewpoint' column in the *Sunday Times*, and the business editorial columns in the *Sunday Telegraph* and *Observer* were classified as predicting a rise or a fall or steadiness/uncertainty/no comment. Each publication was given a class for each month according to which observation, excluding no comments, was most common. Most predictions were for the coming weeks, but some specifically distinguished between the near and the longer term. The results of the exercise are reported in tables 15.1, 15.2 and 15.3. The first two tables report the results for 1990: Table 15.1 relates predictions during a month to the movement of the FT–Actuaries 500 Share Index in that month, while table 15.2 relates the predictions to changes in the market the following month. Where the newspapers distinguished a short-term and a longer-term forecast, the former was used for table 15.1 and the latter for 15.2. (Forecasts made at the start of the year for the year ahead were ignored.) Plainly, interpretation of comments which in some cases were reticent, was required.

The predictions are summarised at the foot of each table. In one sense the predictions *were* accurate; the market fell during 1990 and a substantial majority of the predictions were for a fall – 34 out of 40 observations (table 15.1). However, the predictions did not discriminate between the months in which the falls took place and the months in which the Index rose. The lagged predictions reported in table 15.2 do discriminate more than the current predictions, but 12 of the predictions were for falls in the months in which the market rose,

Table 15.1. *Press predictions, 1990 (1) (predictions during the same month)*

Months when index:	Rise/ fall (%)	Financial Times	Investors Chronicle	Sunday Times	Sunday Telegraph	Observer	Total rises	Total falls	No comment or vague
Rose:									
May	+10.9	fall	fall/rise	fall	rise	rise	2	2	1
June	+1.7	fall	fall	fall	n.c.	fall	0	4	1
October	+1.1	fall/rise	fall	fall	fall	fall	0	4	1
November	+3.4	rise	uncertain	fall	n.c.	fall	1	2	2
December	+0.8	fall	fall/rise	n.c.	n.c.	n.c.	0	1	4
							3	13	9
True		1/4	0/2	0/4	1/2	1/4			
False		3/4	2/2	4/4	1/2	3/4			
Fell:									
January	−3.2	fall	fall	fall	fall	n.c.	0	4	1
February	−3.5	caution/fall	fall	n.c.	n.c.	fall	0	2	3
March	−1.0	fall	fall	fall	n.c.	fall	0	4	1
April	−6.0	fall/steady	fall	n.c.	rise	fall	1	2	2
July	−2.0	fall	fall	fall/rise	rise	fall	1	3	1
August	−8.1	fall	fall	fall	fall/rise	fall/rise	0	3	2
September	−13.8	fall/rise	fall	fall	fall	rise	1	3	1
							3	21	11
True		4/4	7/7	4/4	2/4	4/5			
False		0/4	0/7	0/4	2/4	1/5			

Total predictions for current month						Total
Fall	7	9	8	3	7	34
Rise	1	0	0	3	2	6
No comment/vague	4	3	4	6	3	20
True	5	7	4	3	5	24
False	3	2	4	3	4	16

Note: n.c. = no comment made.

Table 15.2. *Press predictions, 1990 (2) (predictions during the previous month)*

Months when index:	Rise/ fall (%)	Financial Times	Investors Chronicle	Sunday Times	Sunday Telegraph	Observer	Total rises	Total falls	No comment or vague
Rose:									
May	+10.9	fall/steady	fall	n.c.	rise	fall	1	2	2
June	+1.7	fall	rise	fall	rise	fall/rise	2	2	1
October	+1.1	fall/rise	fall	fall	fall/rise	fall	0	3	2
November	+3.4	rise	uncertain	fall	fall	fall	1	3	1
December	+0.8	rise	rise	fall	n.c.	fall	2	2	1
							6	12	7
True		2/3	2/4	0/4	2/3	0/4			
False		1/3	2/4	4/4	1/3	4/4			
Fell:									
January	−3.2	fall	steady	n.c.	rise	rise	2	1	2
February	−3.5	fall	fall	fall	fall/rise	n.c.	0	3	2
March	−1.0	caution	fall	n.c.	n.c.	fall	0	2	3
April	−6.0	fall	rise	fall	n.c.	fall	1	3	1
July	−2.0	fall	fall	fall	n.c.	fall	0	4	1
August	−8.1	fall	fall	fall/rise	rise	fall	1	3	1
September	−13.8	fall	fall	fall	fall/rise	fall	0	4	1
							4	20	11
True		6/6	5/6	4/4	0/2	5/6			
False		0/6	1/6	0/4	2/2	1/6			
Total predictions for current month							Total		
Fall		7	7	8	1	9	32		
Rise		2	3	0	4	1	10		
No comment/vague		3	2	4	7	2	18		
True		8	7	4	2	5	26		
False		1	3	4	3	5	16		

Note: n.c. = no comment made.

compared to 6 predictions which got it right. After sharp falls in August and September 1990 as the Gulf crisis developed, the market rose during each of the last three months of 1990 and again in the first quarter of 1991; generally, the predictions during 1990 did not pick out this change of direction. If the purpose of the advice was to warn shareholders to sell to avoid the fall in share prices during 1990, it had to be followed by advice to buy at the end of 1990 or early in 1991 if the shareholders were not to miss out on the rise in equity prices in 1991.

The Press did predict falling share prices in 1990 and prices did fall. An explanation for this success *could be* that the Press is biased towards predicting falls, and to test this possibility the exercise was re-done for 1985, a year in which the FT–Actuaries 500 Share Index rose by 15.2%. The results are reported in Table 15.3; the exercise is not conclusive – a majority of the predictions were again of falls, but the score was closer – 12 predictions of falls and 10 of rises.

City editors could have a gloomy bias for reasons other than some editors being of a pessimistic turn of mind: perhaps predicting a fall in share prices is more exciting copy, or emphasising the downside may be deemed cautious advice – if readers are induced to sell or hold back from a purchase they can only miss out on a gain; if they are encouraged to buy and prices fall, they lose some of their capital, at least temporarily.

The influence of Press comment

So far the view has been of the Press predicting market movements, but the Press may actually *cause* some market prices to change. The Press is more likely to influence decisions of members of the public than decisions of fund managers, in part because the latter will already have much of the information obtained by journalists from brokers and other sources. It is not possible to assess how influential Press comment is for movements in the market, or even how influential the comments are intended to be: certainly, editors do not expect all their readers to rush out and sell their holdings in response to gloomy predictions. Market makers read the Press; if they expect comments in, for example, the Sunday papers to lead to a wave of selling, they respond by lowering prices on Monday morning. Press comment may influence the timing of price changes with, or without, influencing longer-term movements.

In view of the general under-valuation of equity prices during the post World War II period described in chapter 6, it can be said that the apparently cautious Press advice has not contributed to correcting the undervaluation; it could even have contributed to it. However, it

Table 15.3. *Press predictions, 1985 (predictions during the current month)*

Months when index:	Rise/ fall (%)	Financial Times	Investors Chronicle	Sunday Times	Sunday Telegraph	Observer	Total rises	falls	No comment or vague
Rose:									
January	+3.4	vague	rise	n.c.	rise	n.c.	2	0	3
March	+1.5	fall	fall	n.c.	n.c.	n.c.	0	2	3
April	+4.4	n.c.	fall	n.c.	n.c.	n.c.	0	1	4
May	+2.0	fall	fall	n.c.	n.c.	n.c.	0	2	3
July	+2.1	vague	fall	n.c.	vague	n.c.	0	1	4
August	+6.9	rise	fall	n.c.	n.c.	n.c.	1	1	3
October	+0.3	rise	rise	n.c.	n.c.	n.c.	2	0	3
November	+5.9	rise	fall	rise	rise	n.c.	3	1	1
							8	8	24
True		3/5	2/8	1/1	2/2	0/0	8		
False		2/5	6/8	0/1	0/2	0/0			
Fell:									
February	−1.3	vague	fall	fall	n.c.	n.c.	0	2	3
June	−6.7	n.c.	fall	fall	n.c.	n.c.	0	2	3
September	−3.1	n.c.	rise	vague	vague	n.c.	1	0	4
December	−1.2	rise	vague	n.c.	n.c.	n.c.	1	0	4
							2	4	14
True		0/1	2/3	2/2	0/0	0/0	2		
False		1/1	1/3	0/2	0/0	0/0			
Total predictions for current month							Total		
Fall		2	8	2	0	0	12		
Rise		4	3	1	2	0	10		
n.c./vague		6	1	9	10	12	38		
True		3	4	3	2	0	12		
False		3	7	0	0	0	10		

Note: n.c. = no comment made.

should be noted that although the advice given by editors seems to have had a gloomy tilt, the extensive coverage of news about the stock market and companies in the Press may have encouraged people to buy shares. Also, the comments of journalists could reflect a cautious/ pessimistic slant to the information they obtain from brokers and fund managers and report in their newspapers.

Plainly, the editors of the financial Press do not assume that the EMH operates, otherwise they would not expect to be able to predict market movements as they and their colleagues do. Perusal of City Press comment suggests the question whether City editors often fail to assess whether an event they are reporting or predicting is already in the price of the shares. In effect the Press often, but not always, appears to adopt the convention that the existing state of opinion as expressed in prices is based on the correct summing up of past events, but not of future changes in the state of the economy. These will cause prices to change, so, if City editors can 'beat the gun' in identifying changes in the economy or changes affecting a company, they will be able to predict share price movements. Also, there is a more or less complete absence in the Press of references to, or use of, mathematical techniques apart from charts – editors do not refer to betas when forecasting movements of the prices of the shares of companies.

Part V
Conclusions

16 Keynes's propositions, the Efficient Markets Hypothesis and bubbles

Keynes's propositions

Do the results of the survey of fund managers' practices reported in part III and the evidence described in parts II and IV confirm Keynes's propositions? The propositions which are summarised at the end of chapter 1 are considered in turn.

Proposition 1: It is difficult or impossible to forecast long-term yields on many investments.

Survey result: Analysts' forecasts of profits are generally limited to a two-year horizon. Given these short-term forecasts, implicit, relative, expected, long-term rates of growth of profits for companies can be deduced from share prices, but for most companies assessments of relative long-term, rates of growth of profits are hazardous and are not *quantified* by analysts. This absence of *quantified* estimates of long-run profits is consistent with Keynes's view about the uncertainty of future returns on investments.

Proposition 2: Investors assume the current state of affairs will continue indefinitely except in so far as there are definite reasons for expecting a change

Survey result: Fund managers do assume that some aspects of the current state of affairs will *continue*, a major world recession, war, or stock market crash were not expected and no one explicitly acted on the assumption that there would be a repeat of the 1970s inflation. Similarly, at a micro level, the chemical and engineering industries were expected to continue to be cyclical and the patent system for pharmaceuticals to allow some pharmaceutical companies to be very profitable.

It would not be true to say that managers assume the current state of affairs will continue *indefinitely*. In practice, many of them focus on what they expect will happen during the next six to twelve months. They hope that they will foresee and act upon new events beyond that time span nearer the time of the events.

Keynes's suggestion, that investors expect prices to be broadly stable in the short term and so they only need to consider price movements a short time ahead because they will have the option of selling their shares without incurring large losses, if true prior to 1987, was shaken by the crash that year.

Proposition 3: Investors assume that existing market prices are based on a correct summing up of future prospects

Survey result: The managers seemed very wary about the level of existing market prices and were seeking to exploit future changes in prices. However, some managers operate rules which show that they believe that within limits market prices are correct.

Much, though certainly not all, of the Press comment about the general level of share prices seems to assume that the existing market prices are based on a correct summing up of past events and that if the writer can forecast changes in the economy he will also be able to forecast share prices.

Proposition 4: Investors endeavour to conform with the behaviour of the majority or average

Survey result: There was clear evidence that many fund managers did take account of the *allocation* of investments to classes of assets by their competitors, and an important explanation for this behaviour was to limit the extent of any failure to match average performance. Nevertheless, through time, institutions do make important changes in asset allocation. Managers do not seek to copy the share selection of other funds, but weightings for industries in the market index do constrain their selection to a limited extent.

Proposition 5: Professional investors are preoccupied with foreseeing changes in the conventional basis of valuation a short time ahead of the general public, not with making superior long-term forecasts of the probable yields of investments.

Survey result: The nature of the market has changed since 1936; institutions now account for more than 80% of stock market turnover. Few managers spend time directly guessing what the public (private shareholders) will do in the future. Although they do not spend much time assessing what private shareholders will do, fund managers do try to foresee changes in investment strategy which other managers will make. One approach to this is to analyse information to assess where the market is undervaluing or overvaluing assets taking account of both short-term and long-term prospects. (This is close to Keynes's own strategy of looking for bargains – shares whose intrinsic value exceeded their market values: see chapter 13 above.) The assumption is that other managers will recognise the undervaluation later and will buy the asset. In some instances managers accept that a share or market is relatively undervalued, but delay purchases because they believe that other managers will also delay purchases until, for example, recovery of profits is nearer. So far as I could judge, the efforts of most fund managers and analysts are weighted towards identifying assets which are undervalued rather than towards guessing what other fund managers will do next.

It is very difficult indeed to assess and quantify the long-term prospects for many companies and hence what the companies are really worth, and this is one explanation why investment managers concentrate on quantifying relatively short-term prospects. In my view Keynes's description early in chapter 12 of *The General Theory* is apt:

> It would be foolish, in forming our expectations, to attach great weight to matters which are very uncertain. It is reasonable, therefore, to be guided to a considerable degree by the facts about which we feel somewhat confident [recent and expected profits over the short-term horizon] even though they may be less decisively relevant to the issue than other facts about which our knowledge is vague and scanty [profits over the long term]. For this reason the facts of the existing situation enter, in a sense disproportionately, into the formation of our long-term expectations [share prices]. (CW, VII, p. 148)

One explanation for fluctuations in share prices is that from time to time short-term results and prospects have a disproportionate impact on investment decisions and prices. This works at times to reduce the prices of the shares of companies whose profits fall or are low and to inflate prices for firms with good profit records.

Proposition 6: Reliance on conventions when taking decisions . . . can impart stability . . . at times, and at other times . . . instability – especially when circumstances change

Survey result: The survey suggested how this proposition could operate in practice. Firstly, effects inducing instability: as many fund managers attempt to match approximately the asset allocation of competitors, once a movement begins a bandwagon effect could ensue and result in instability. Secondly, effects inducing stability: the expectation that historical levels of yields, price/earnings ratios, etc, will persist and/or that share prices will move within a range, tends, in the absence of shocks, to result in stability. In addition, these practices could also result in a persistent undervaluation of shares.

Proposition 7: The instability of the market will increase as the proportion of shares owned by ignorant individuals (unprofessional investors) increases. However, the practice of professional investors treating the market as a beauty contest may lead to instability

Survey result: So far there is no statistical evidence that the replacement of private investors by fund managers has stabilised prices on the stock market, though it is possible that any tendency towards greater stability caused by the switch of assets from private investors to fund managers is offset by other changes, such as greater macro-economic instability, causing greater volatility of share prices.

An application of the beauty contest relates to themes or fashions. Managers are concerned to foresee themes of fashions which will drive the market whether the themes are based on fads, or on changing assessments of fundamentals (e.g., greater realisation of the importance of brands; an example of news during the period of the study was that the UK government would join the ERM; or new products or services). Some managers are engaged in trying to be one step ahead of other managers in going liquid or investing funds or increasing their weighting in particular overseas markets. Some of these attempts are based on the hope of managers that they have greater foresight or quicker responses than other managers, while other attempts are assessments of the mood of investors and guesses at what fund managers will do next.

Keynes did not describe the role of market makers in his analysis of the stock market. Another explanation for the instability of the stock market is that spot share markets are to an extent inevitably unstable; market makers have to clear their books in a vast range of securities and they create business by moving prices.

Conclusion

In brief, Keynes's analysis of the activities of investors is relevant to the contemporary stock market. My assessment is that anticipation of moves by other fund managers plays a part in decision making, but that, in aggregate, the efforts of fund managers are weighted towards identifying assets which are undervalued. Fund managers are also influenced by conventions, but the *relative* importance of conventions could not be assessed. This study was not made at a time of financial crisis in the sense that stock market prices did not fall very heavily, nor was there a sustained boom in prices; the basis of decision making by fund managers could be different at such times.

The Efficient Markets Hypothesis

As noted in chapter 2, it is not possible to test the EMH directly because fundamental values cannot be measured. Institutional investors now dominate the market. How do their activities and the functioning of the market conform to the assumptions underlying the EMH?

Probabilities

Managers make very little, if any, attempt to determine probabilities for alternative estimates of the earnings of companies. Apart from the uncertainty about the prospects for individual events such as a deep recession, attempts to forecast far ahead and attach probabilities to the forecasts are thwarted by the many dimensions in which uncertainty operates: the diversity of events which can affect earnings includes the policies adopted by UK and foreign governments, developments of technology, changes in consumer tastes and management changes at companies. Explicit probabilities are not attached to alternative economic scenarios by most analysts and fund managers.

No one doubts that it is impossible to predict the long-term growth of profits for a company accurately. Nevertheless, some companies are more likely than others to achieve rapid growth of profits over the long term and so fund managers can attempt to rank companies according to their prospects relative to the prices of the companies' shares and implicitly they do this when they select shares to buy – at least they have two categories of companies, companies whose shares they hold or plan to buy and those whose shares they do not hold or plan to sell. Managers often vary the amount they invest in different companies according to their forecasts of returns and their confidence in the companies achieving the forecast returns. (Their confidence could reflect implicit vague assessments of probability distributions of possible returns, but such assessments would be based on a limited range of existing information and be very inexact.) In practice, the investment decisions made by investors are not based on a ranking of all investments. Investors, even the largest insurance companies, have not got the resources to assess all possible investments and they have to make a selection of which securities to assess. Many investors make similar selections (for example, limiting their choice to large companies or the largest 100 companies) and this process of selection could distort the relative prices of shares.

One incentive largely to ignore possibilities with low probabilities, such as a very deep and protracted slump, is that if a fund holds some bonds as a precaution for this possibility, its performance will lag behind other funds investing in equities, if in the event, a deep and protracted recession does not occur (see p. 106).

Rational behaviour

Another practical flaw in the Rational Expectations/EMH is that not all of the decisions taken by investors are rational. Irrational influences, hope, fear and so on, do play a part: the oft-quoted statement that the market is driven by alternating bouts of greed and fear sums up the position. The words 'judgement' and 'feel' are often used by investors and commentators. One view of judgement is that it is an intuitive assessment taking account of all the factors bearing on a decision. In practice, judgement and feel for the market are based on a sifting of information and the sifting is affected by what is perceived to be happening in the market and the economy. If it were possible to asses what shares are really worth, irrational elements in forming judgement and determining confidence would not be as important but, in practice, what shares are really worth is uncertain. Even those, if they exist, who can themselves ignore or compensate for irrational elements in their own decision taking know that the judgement of others is affected by them, and that market prices will be affected, so that irrational decisions could affect their own investment decisions. Certainly, irrational elements enter into the investment decisions of some individuals, but it has not been possible to assess how important they are at an aggregate level or the extent to which fund managers' decisions are affected by irrational impulses. Many of the fund managers interviewed certainly attempted to base all their decisions on rational assessments of prospects.

Re-balancing portfolios

Although managers respond to changes in the relative prices of securities, there are constraints on their switching holdings to re-balance their portfolios because of conventions and rules to which they adhere. For much of the time many institutional investors have limited scope for re-balancing their portfolios. For example, if equity and bond prices fall and are considered cheap, funds which are already fully or near fully invested in equities and bonds can do little to take advantage of the position. They could enter into forward purchases through futures contracts, but institutions are generally reluctant to do this because of the uncertainty about the future – an unexpected political crisis or event or the vagaries of the market could always drive equities and bonds even lower.

Conclusion

Important assumptions under-pinning the EMH simply do not apply in practice.

Bubbles

Box 5 outlines explanations for movements in the prices of the shares of small companies during the 1980s, where several forces interacted to create this bubble which was not on as great a scale as some historic bubbles. In reality, the combination and interaction of forces is much more complex than theories based on rational behaviour and noise trading by less well-informed investors allow. Extrapolation of trends and buying by knowledgeable buyers in the expectation that prices will be pushed further and further above values indicated by fundamentals play at most a limited role. (Theories of the causes of bubbles were outlined in chapter 3.)

One explanation for bubbles attributes them to the activities of 'uninformed' or 'ignorant individuals', and of 'professionals' investing to take advantage of the investment decisions of less well-informed investors. This study suggests that although uninformed investors may directly (and indirectly by buying unit trusts) play a part in creating bubbles and bursts, these activities are only part of the explanation. The reliance by fund managers on benchmarks, the importance some of them attach to sentiment and their overwhelming share of the market suggests they too play a part in creating bubbles. Also, bubbles occur in the commercial property market where the general public does not participate.

Many buyers of the shares of small companies in the late 1980s considered they were acquiring attractive investments. They misread the underlying economic and industrial circumstances. The long boom of the 1980s had provided a favourable economic background for firms and particularly small firms – the initial 1980s boom in share prices and, from 1985, the relative outperformance of the shares of small companies reflected favourable economic developments, improving fundamentals – but prices overshot and later fell back. Some investors may have extrapolated the growth of dividends or share prices, or acted as noise traders. (A reason why some fund managers backed certain small companies growing by takeovers was that they had been impressed by the performance of the conglomerate companies Hanson and BTR. In the event, many, but not all, of these concoctions ran into difficulties in the 1990/1991 recession and some did not survive.) Similarly, *with hindsight*, it is clear that during the commercial property bubbles described in chapter 7 businessmen and investors misread fundamentals; the initial rise in asset prices was triggered by increasing

Box 5   Smaller companies

The movements of the returns on the shares of smaller companies, shown in figure 16.1, provide an interesting case study of many of the forces determining movements of share prices. Between 1985 and 1988 the Hoare Govett Smaller Companies Index showed total returns one third more than the 84% return shown by the FT–Actuaries Index. In 1987 and 1988 the Smaller Companies Index showed a return of 21.1% and 16.5% compared to 7.9% and 11.2% for the FT–Actuaries Index. In the following two years the relative performance of the Smaller Companies Index was much worse; while the return for the FT–Actuaries Index was 35.6% in 1989 and − 9.8% in 1990, the Smaller Companies Index returns were 10.8% in 1989 and − 23.1% in 1990. Piecing together the information and evidence reported in earlier chapters the sequence of events appears to have been:

(a) Evidence emerged in the 1970s that shares of smaller companies, on average, outperformed the market indices. One explanation for this outperformance was that they were undervalued at the start of the period used for comparison.

(b) During the 1970s and 1980s unit trusts specialising in investment in smaller companies were set up and did well. Also, many other unit trusts and institutions not specialising in investment in small companies invested some part of their funds in smaller companies.

(c) During the 1980s small firms and companies became fashionable. There was political interest in and support for their development and this may have focused the attention of investors on the shares of small companies.

(d) Partly, at least, because of the increased demand for their shares, smaller companies, on average, continued to match and then outperform the broad indices during the 1980s.

(e) Investors seeing the outperformance by shares of small companies continued to invest in small companies and unit trusts specialising in small companies.

(f) The recession of 1990 triggered by very high real interest rates adversely affected smaller companies because of their concentration on the UK market and relatively high borrowing in the UK. In addition, a higher proportion of small firms were exposed to trades hit hardest by recession.

(g) The adverse fundamentals in 1989/1990 led to underperformance by smaller companies' shares and this pricked the bubble in them. Some institutions withdrew from investing in smaller companies. The increasing popularity of tracker funds at the end of the 1980s contributed to the outperformance of index stocks relative to the others not included among the companies used for compiling the main indices – the smaller companies.

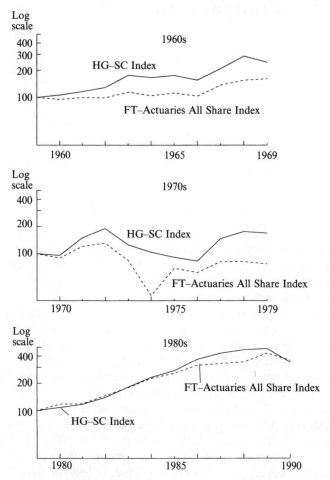

**Figure 16.1 The returns on the shares of smaller companies.
Source: Hoare Govett, 1990.**

demand for space and rents, but again property prices overshot and
later fell. Many of the property companies which collapsed in 1990–92
or had to be rescued by bankers were led and advised by people
considered to be property experts. Some investors in property may have
extrapolated the *growth* of rents.

The initial rise in the prices of shares of small companies and
property were triggered by economic developments. Perhaps increases
in asset prices set off by more capricious influences also have a habit of
overshooting, or do so on some occasions. The underlying explanation
for bubbles is the uncertainty about what the shares of companies and
properties are really worth, since even experts rely on extrapolation of
past trends in the growth of profits dividends and rents.

17 Implications of the study

Why is it difficult to outwit the market?

The fact that Keynes was unable to make much success of moving in and out of the market during the 1920s and 1930s is instructive. Instrumental investment was less developed and a majority of investors may have been less well-informed about the economy as a whole than present-day fund managers. In 1990, institutional investors were playing the market against each other and all the competitors had access to similar economic and industrial forecasts. In total, attempts to outperform the market by fund managers by active trading is a negative sum game; if some managers win, others must lose more than the winners gain because of the transaction costs.

Share prices should discount the future, so at the top of the boom prices should discount the impending slow down or recession and subsequent cyclical changes. At the peak of a boom it is difficult to predict how severe the slow down or recession will be. If, as in 1990, the recession becomes unexpectedly severe, unless the investor recognises this in advance of other investors, share prices will have fallen before he sells. Of course, some investors and forecasters foresee events and developments, but some of those who forecast the difficulties for the economy in 1990 had been forecasting an economic crisis since the mid 1980s or even earlier and did not expect the boom circa 1988. Another complicating factor is that the *contents and timing* of decisions of the authorities are often difficult to predict. At the beginning of 1990, why should rational investors have been expecting that the government would pursue a high exchange rate/interest rate policy before an election to the point of allowing a deep recession to develop?

Unexpected changes occur in companies as well as economies. An investor may sell a share in response to poor performance but the management of the company may change and achieve a good performance or the company may be taken over at a premium. Most investors have little information on which to assess the new managers of a company. Also, the extent of the swing in share prices is sometimes excessive and therefore difficult to predict: the growth of aggregate profits may be cut more than expected for a year or two, but for many companies growth is likely to be resumed after that. If, as seems to be the case, and this is an important point, many changes in share prices are irrational in the sense that they do not reflect known changes in fundamentals, they are always likely to be difficult to predict. But this does provide investors with an opportunity to fish among companies whose share prices have fallen heavily.

In chapter 13 it was suggested that Keynes, at least at times, took too optimistic a view of future developments and in chapter 15 there was tentative evidence that at least some City editors have a pessimistic bias. If such biases apply, the individuals concerned will be handicapped in playing the market or when advising others to do so. Similarly, investors may become committed to managements of companies and managements may gain from that support, but it may make for difficulty in selling shares.

One ingredient of the superior long-term performance of certain investment houses seems to lie in their contacts with managers of companies and the information they obtain about companies. Information obtained has to be sifted, assessed and interpreted and so availability of information does not alone guarantee superior long-term performance.

Tracker funds

In response to the mediocre record of fund managers relative to the market indices, tracker funds which mimic the indices have become popular, particularly with pension funds which can negotiate very low management charges for investments placed in these tracker funds. Until recently, unit trust groups which offered tracker funds have made the standard initial charge and levied a lower annual management charge, but private investors did not obtain the full benefits of the lower management and transaction costs incurred by such funds. Certain investment trusts which follow the tracker principle offer private investors a convenient entrée to such funds, but because the discount of investment trust share prices to the value of their share holdings fluctuates, the investor cannot be sure to match the index the investment trust is tracking over the period he holds the shares. Of course tracker funds would not suit all investors in unit trusts. Some investment managers outperform the index and some investors believe they can pick these managers or hope to do so, or they want the excitement of their investments having a chance of beating the index; nevertheless, there seems to be a gap in the unit trust market for more tracker funds with low charges.[1]

Fama (1991) has claimed that the massive American investment in tracker funds is the result of research on efficient markets and even suggests that this 'is a premier case where academic research has affected real-world practice'. To this writer Fama seems to exaggerate. It is inevitable that, in aggregate, professional fund managers cannot beat the market, taking one year with another, because they control such a large fraction of it and some other investors have inside knowledge which they can exploit. Directors, employees, suppliers, customers and competitors have access to unpublished information which from time to time has implications for the value of a company's shares, and gives these investors an advantage. Despite these handicaps, some managers do beat the indices and tracker funds over long periods. (Recent assessments of the relative performance of UK tracker funds may be misleading because, during a period in which these funds gain market share, a disproportionate share of investment will be channelled towards index stocks, thereby inflating their relative prices.) The trick is to select those managers who beat the index; so far, financial theory has provided little guidance on how to do this.

Background

In chapter 12 of *The General Theory*, Keynes questioned the basis of stock market valuations, related fluctuations in investment in real assets – property, plant and machinery – to volatile stock market prices, and advocated greater government control of investment. Keynes was not alone in advocating greater government intervention in the economy: in *The Middle Way*, published in 1938, Harold Macmillan proposed a 'wide extension of social enterprise and control in the sphere of [providing] minimum human needs'.

From the 1930s until the 1970s the Keynesian/Middle Way consensus held; the expansion of the public sector by nationalisation and the creation of the National Health Service during the early post-war period were not rolled back. The government intervened to control aggregate demand and encourage industrial investment through the operation of various controls during the early post-war period and then by manipulating tax allowances. During the 1970s, rapid inflation, slow growth and the defensive/intransigent stances adopted by trade unions led to the collapse of the consensus.

The economic drawbacks of centralisation described by Hayek (1944) and Friedman's (1969) analysis of the limitations on government intervention to regulate aggregate demand and inflation were accepted by the Conservative Government which was elected in 1979. The money supply would be controlled, the budget would be balanced and the allocation of resources would be left to the market. In the event, the money supply was not controlled and the Lawson credit boom from 1986 to 1988 ended in recession and an annual inflation rate of 10% in 1990. Although the growth of labour productivity in manufacturing industries speeded up, much of Britain's lack of industrial competitiveness compared to Japan and Germany persisted.

The vagaries of the foreign exchange rate for the dollar during the 1980s and the stock market crash of 1987 at least momentarily shook faith in the reliability of markets, but the crash was not immediately followed by a recession. If share prices boom, bubble and burst, how can this result in an efficient allocation of resources? In 1990, the failure of many fund managers to pick out long-term winners was witnessed by the appointment of receivers to a succession of companies whose shares had been high flyers during the 1980s. Some comparative studies have claimed that Britain's arch-competitors, Japan and Germany, operate in a different financial and corporate environment and that companies based in those countries are less dependent upon the stock market than their UK counterparts. Finally, the persistence of the recession in 1991 led the US and UK governments to accept the case for fiscal intervention to stabilise aggregate demand – both governments took fiscal measures to stabilise aggregate demand and in the US the proposed measures included tax incentives to bring forward investment.

What this study has shown

This study has reviewed the practices of fund managers and the operation of the stock market. Claims have been made that the stock market is 'efficient' and that it 'correctly reflects all relevant information in determining security prices'; during the 1980s such claims backed-up fashionable laissez-faire policies and deregulation of the financial system. Although these claims are based on a wide range of limited statistical tests, there are serious qualifications to the assessment that the stock market correctly values securities in terms of fundamentals, however these are defined, or reflects what shares are really worth. Firstly, assumptions which under-pin the EMH do not apply to the stock market (see chapter 16). Secondly, the short-term volatility of share prices cannot be justified by changes in fundamentals (see chapter 4). Thirdly, the stock market has undervalued equities for long periods (see chapter 6) and fourthly, because the use of, and reliance on conventions affect share prices (see chapter 16). From time to time there are booms, bubbles and bursts but, even more importantly, the volatility of share prices shows that the prediction of movements in share prices is a very hit and miss affair. The stock market is not clinically efficient, as the term EMH would imply. Keynes's analysis of the determination of stock market prices in the face of uncertainty still provides an important explanation for the erratic movements of share prices and the persistent undervaluation of equities.[2]

The extent to which fluctuations in share prices lead to instability of investment and the economy is difficult to assess and has not been a focus of this book. During the post 1970 period, macroeconomic fluctuations have often originated with changes in consumption rather than industrial and commercial investment. Certainly, changes in the economy have influenced share prices, but share price movements may have reinforced changes in investment in new assets through the links specified by Keynes (and which are described in chapter 1) and by altering the confidence of managers and some consumers. Also, the undervaluation of equities will have dampened investment.

The operation of the stock market

The 1980s were an easy decade for fund managers. Both stock market and commercial property investments provided high returns by historical criteria; whether or not fund managers added value, investors obtained high returns. The easy market conditions of the 1980s did not persist into 1990 and investment returns in real terms during the 1990s are unlikely to match those of the 1980s. The question of how fund managers add value is likely to be asked more insistently at a time when the rate of return on investments is lower. Fund managers do enable investors to achieve a spread of investments and in the case of managed funds they provide expertise in moving funds between categories of investment in response to changes in economic circumstances. In addition, fund managers have some protection because of the tax advantages for investors of investing through institutions rather than by direct investment in companies.

It is outside the scope of this book to assess alternative systems to the stock market for allocating capital to companies or to assess policies to supplement the stock market's role in allocating capital. However, some aspects of the operation of the stock market seem inefficient and call for comment. These inefficiencies may, in part, be a hang-over from the regime of fixed commissions when brokers competed by providing fund managers with data and company analyses. One danger of brokers providing analyses of information about companies is that their primary motivation is to get clients to buy or sell shares, and this might introduce a bias towards dwelling on the strong or the weak points in a company's record. Also, there sems to be too much replication of analyses of information at a rather superficial level and there is some evidence that the existing analyses of published accounting data are not perceptive (see Gwilliam and Russell, 1991). The point can be put another way – it might be more efficient for a small number of fund managers and/or brokers to develop greater expertise in analysing published accounts and expert systems for using information published by companies and from other sources. One way to develop this expertise would be for the largest fund management groups to do it in-house. The weakness of this arrangement, and an advantage of the present system of stockbrokers providing analyses, is that if a few fund managers develop the systems the results would not be available to other fund managers (the public good argument). An alternative is for fund managers collectively to finance firms set up to analyse accounts and develop expert systems.

Plainly there are limitations on the use of expert systems to deal with the vast flow of information from companies and elsewhere, and computer models cannot easily use the impressionistic assessments which analysts obtain at meetings with management. The advantages of expert systems are that they are not affected by any emotional commitments to companies or commitments to earlier decisions. The increasing use of such systems may in time reduce duplication of effort in interpreting news, and dampen the tendency for there to be an exaggerated response to news.

Stakes in companies

Most fund managers shy away from taking large stakes in companies, although there are notable exceptions, such as the M&G group. The bad results of many widely diversified conglomerate companies suggests that it would be disastrous for fund managers to get involved in the management of a wide range of companies operating in different industries. Nor would it be practicable for most institutions to take large stakes in giant companies such as ICI and GEC. Nevertheless, there are examples of institutions playing a very constructive role in the affairs of companies in which they have large stakes and adding value in this way. An outstanding example is the Wallenberg Skandinaviska Enskilda Bank which has held stakes giving it control of many of the leading Swedish industrial companies; but genius in this activity is difficult to emulate.

To fulfil a supervisory role, institutions would have to develop a knowledge of industrial management which at present most of them lack. Where they hold large stakes in companies, the role of institutions is not to take management decisions, but they do have to be in a position to assess management. The appointment of the chief executives of companies is crucial, and one cause for concern given the importance of management and Britain's industrial performance is whether the selections made are satisfactory. Creative industrial management needs much more than the imposition of tight financial controls; it requires the ability to see industrial opportunities and to appoint and inspire managers and employees. Although financial expertise is important, it can be hired much more readily than technical knowledge, which is highly specific to firms and trades.

One procedure is for institutions to rely upon the separation of the role of chairman (whose principal functions are to monitor the performance of the chief executive and supervise the long-term strategy of a company) and that of chief executive (who manages the company's operations) and 'outside directors' of companies. With these arrangements much depends on the choices of chairmen and the outside directors, and one danger with a rapid spread of this system is that those chosen will not have sufficient experience. Chairmen could have itchy fingers to interfere in management and could appoint weak chief executives to retain or increase their own authority; outside directors may not be able to intervene constructively. This is less likely to happen where the chairman and outside directors are executive directors of other companies.

The institutions' role in appointing managements is of great importance for improving the performance of companies and the return on investments. One way of replacing management is through takeovers by successful management teams. However, new ways are needed for institutions to identify talented, knowledgeable and experienced managers and aid their promotion.

Short-termism

Short-termism and the failure to take large stakes in companies and build up industrial expertise are closely related. If institutions hold shares for long periods they have an incentive to obtain more information about the companies in which they hold stakes and to monitor and supervise managements, and each institution can only do this for a limited number of holdings – hence the link with large share stakes.

At the start of a discussion of short-termism the problems facing the investment managers of institutions have to be recognised. It was shown in chapter 5 that real dividends increased very slowly between 1926 and 1980. Institutions have a duty to provide returns for investors and are under intense competitive pressure to do so. If the growth of real profits and real dividends has been very slow, the fault lies with the quality of industrial management and/or labour taking too high a share of value added – put simply, wages have been too high. Also, the erratic economic policies pursued by UK governments have contributed to economic instability. Failure to appreciate the effects of policies and the position of the economy contributed to the booms of 1973 and 1988 and the recessions of 1980 and 1990, but political vacillation over economic objectives also played a part. For example, in 1987–8 the priority seems to have been to reduce unemployment but by 1990 controlling inflation was given absolute priority.

Two forces propel fund managers to focus on the short term. Firstly, short-term performance over less than five years is used in assessing the performance of fund managers and, secondly, it is very difficult to foresee what will happen over a five-to-ten year span of time. Nevertheless, there is a case for some companies/fund managers to focus more on the longer term:

(1) at present, such a vast amount of attention and analysis is concentrated on the near term and news, that interpreting the effects of news must be a negative sum game for many fund managers. Yet dividends and profits over the next two years account for less than 10 and 20% respectively of average share prices;

(2) there may be a gap in the market for institutions to concentrate on longer-term prospects and so minimise trading costs. That is not to say the investment houses at present ignore the longer term; some houses search for long-term growth stocks and some act contrary to what they regard as fads or fashions; nevertheless, the weight of effort is concentrated on the short term. Nor is there an easy recipe for assessing the long-term prospects for companies.

There are some managers who are good at aggressive fund management, have a combination of good access to information, flexibility to reverse past decisions, and a nose for assessing the mood of other investors, interpreting accounts or assessing managers. At least for a time, some fund managers make a success of active management policies but, as it is a negative sum game, fund managers, other investors, and the Press should take a cautious view of the likely results of themselves or their readers playing this game. Investors should ask themselves whether they really have an advantage in acquiring news about the economy or companies before other investors or for analysing the effects of the news. In practice, brokers and fund managers obtain information from companies before it is available to most of the public, as there is a lag of a day or so before information is reported in the Press and much of the information given to brokers and fund managers at meetings is not published. If investors do not have an advantage, they are unlikely to gain by aggressive trading or rapid turnover of their holdings.

Final conclusion

It may seem surprising, but there is controversy about the value of the insights into the operation of the stock market that Keynes provided. In his eulogy for Professor Harry Markowitz on the occasion of Markowitz being awarded the Nobel Prize for economics, Professor Brealey of the London Business School went out of his way to claim that 'Keynes did no service to economics with his dismissive quips about stock market investment' (Brealey, 1991). The conclusion of this study is that Keynes did provide important insights which apply to the operation of the contemporary stock market, and to the explanation of the erratic movement of asset prices. Uncertainty about the future, which was the focus of Keynes's analysis, and the reaction of agents to that uncertainty also undermine the apparent virtuosity of the finance theory that Professor Brealey finds so convincing. Much of modern applied finance theory is devoted to testing the realism of the EMH and these tests have proliferated to the extent where they are in the academic equivalent of an asset price bubble. So far, investment managers have found rather limited scope for the practical application of modern finance theory. The interesting and important problems are to improve methods of managing the economy (which was Keynes's principal interest), of industrial management (which was not a subject area where Keynes was expert), of monitoring industrial managers, and of assessing the long-term prospects for companies and the value of their shares.

18 Are equities undervalued?

The comparisons of returns in chapter 6 show that equities have been undervalued through much of the post-war period relative to other financial assets. The return on investments in equities, made up of dividends and capital appreciation, has exceeded the return on gilts or investments placed with building societies by a very large margin. Were equities still undervalued in 1991? Answering this question in September 1991 provided the acid test for assessing the value of shares.[1]

Instead of focusing on the prospects for share prices over the next year or two, as most Press and other commentators do, in this chapter the movement of dividends and share prices in the long term, over the next ten years, is considered. In fact, providing certain assumptions are made, only two variables have to be forecast to predict the return on equities. The assumptions are that:

(1) profits are inflation proofed, which implies that companies can increase prices and profits in line with inflation;
(2) profits earned in 1990 were on trend;
(3) the proportion of earnings which companies distribute as dividends will not change;
(4) tax rates will not change
(5) yields on equities will not change, which means share prices will move in step with dividends

Given these five assumptions, the only variables which have to be forecast to predict the nominal return on equities are the rate of inflation and the after-tax rate of profits companies will earn on the profits they retain and reinvest. In the long term it is the rate of growth of dividends that determines the nominal return on equities; the growth of dividends is determined in turn by the rate of inflation and the profitability of retained earnings.

If inflation is at 3%, it follows from the assumptions that profits, dividends and share prices will keep pace. Also, the effects on dividends and share prices of companies earning an after-tax rate of profits

Table 18.1. *Annual returns on equities (given certain assumptions[a])*

Annual inflation rate
(%)

	annual after-tax yield on retained earnings(%)		
	0	5	10
	expected annual return on equities(%)		
0	4.6	6.9	9.3
1	5.7	8.0	10.4
3	7.8	10.1	12.5
5	9.9	12.3	14.7
10	15.1	17.6	20.2

Note: [a] The assumptions underlying this table are described in the text.

of, say, 5% on their retained profits can be estimated. On 21 September 1991 the dividend yield on the FT–Actuaries 500 Share Index was 4.62%, retained profits represented 4.14% of share prices and the earnings yield was 8.76%. In the first year, earnings will rise by 5% of retained earnings, 4.14%, which equals 0.207% of share prices. With a constant pay-out ratio, the increased earnings will will lead to an increase in dividends in proportion to the ratio of dividends to earnings: 4.14:8.76 of the increase in earnings of 0.207%, equals 0.098%. With a constant dividend yield this increase in dividends will result in a proportional increase in share prices of $0.098 \div 4.62 \times 100$ equals 2.12%. The return on equities in the first year will be the dividend 4.72%[2] and capital appreciation 2.12%, a total return of 6.94%. If inflation is 3%, the nominal return will be 10.1%.

The nominal return on equities given alternative rates of inflation and profits on retained earnings is illustrated in table 18.1. Transaction costs are ignored. The annual return of 10.1% given 3% inflation and after-tax profits of 5% on retained profits is shown in row 3 column 2.

The most difficult assumptions made for this exercise concern profits. Firstly, it is blandly assumed that profits were on trend in 1990; if profits were above trend, then some downward revision of the estimates of dividend growth would be required. One reason why reported profits were overstated in 1990 was that the underlying UK inflation rate was about 7%. On the other side, the UK economy was moving into a recession in 1990 which reduced profits in 1990 (and would further reduce profits of many companies in 1991). Here, it is heroically assumed that these opposing influences cancel out. Implicitly, it is assumed that profits are not going to be eroded by an intensification of international competition or persistently deflationary

Table 18.2. *Comparative gross returns (with inflation at 3% per annum from September 1991 and before tax and any management or transaction costs) (%)*

	Deposits		Gilts[a]				Equities			
	yield	returns	yield	capital gain	returns	cumulative returns	yield	capital gain	returns	cumulative returns
Sept. 1991	9.4		9.4				4.6			
Year to										
Sept. 1992	8.0	8.7	8.0	8.5[b]	18.7	18.7	4.86	5.56	10.7	11
Sept. 1993	8.0	8.0	8.0	0	8.0	28.2	5.13	5.56	11.0	23
Sept. 1994	8.0	8.0	8.0	0	8.0	38.5	5.41	5.56	11.3	37
Sept. 1995	8.0	8.0	8.0	0	8.0	49.5	5.71	5.56	11.6	53
Sept. 1996	8.0	8.0	8.0	0	8.0	61.5	6.03	5.56	11.9	71
Sept. 1997	8.0	8.0	8.0	0	8.0	74.4	6.37	5.56	12.3	92
Sept. 1998	8.0	8.0	8.0	0	8.0	88.4	6.72	5.56	12.7	116
Sept. 1999	8.0	8.0	8.0	0	8.0	103.4	7.10	5.56	13.1	144
Sept. 2000	8.0	8.0	8.0	0	8.0	119.7	7.50	5.56	13.5	177

Notes: [a] The yield shown at September 1991 was for government bonds with more than 15 years and less than 20 years to run. [b] For an unredeemable stock the capital gain would be 17.5%. For a stock with, say, 17 years to run, the capital gain which would depend upon the rate at which returns are discounted, would be about 8.5%.
Source: author's calculations.

policies, including policies which provide no relief from recession, to control inflation. If profits do not increase, the outlook for future investment in the UK will be bleak. Secondly, there is evidence that in the past the profits earned on retained earnings have been very low (see chapter 6); nevertheless, 5% after tax seems a cautious estimate for the future, as most companies have a much higher target rate of return or cut off level for new investments. If inflation is in the range 3 to 5%, the trend nominal return on equities will be 10.1 to 12.3%. There is another possible catch in the assumptions if the rate of inflation were to increase: in the 1970s companies had difficulty in increasing profits and dividends in line with very rapid inflation.

A comparison of returns

Table 18.2 compares possible gross returns on alternative investments (*before* tax and any management or transaction costs) to the year 2000. The table starts with yields in September 1991 and assumes that:

1   the annual rate of inflation from September 1991 will be 3% per annum;
2   real dividends will increase by 2.5% per annum, approximately equivalent to assuming a return of 5% on ploughed-back profits, together with a constant pay-out ratio;
3   the real rate of interest on both deposits and bonds is 5% – on the basis of very long-term historical experience this is high, but is lower than the projected real returns on equities.

Given these assumptions, the nominal rate of interest can be expected to fall, and this will result in substantial capital gains on gilt-edged (government bonds). Even so, the cumulative return on equities will exceed that on bonds by September 1995 and this is based on a cautious projection of real dividends increasing at 2½% a year. If real dividends were assumed to increase by 5% a year, the cumulative return on equities by September 1995 would be 70% compared with 53% if real dividends were growing at 2½%. Also, the projected fall in yields on deposits and gilts will be likely to trigger a fall in yields on and an increase in the prices of equities.

If the inflation rate were to average out at less than 3% during the rest of the 1990s that would provide a further boost to the return on gilts and reduce the return on equities, but a faster rate of inflation seems at least as likely as a rate lower than 3% per annum. Plainly, the trend rate of inflation is both very important for such calculations and is uncertain. If the average rate of inflation were to fall from 3% to zero and the yield on gilts were to fall in step from 8% to 5%, the price of irredeemable gilts would rise by 60%, and gilts with between 15 and 20 years to run by approximately 30%.

So far these tentative calculations suggest that UK equities are under-valued in September 1991 relative to investments in fixed interest securities and deposits. The equity market is made up of sectors and can be segmented between groups such as international food and drink companies and pharmaceutical companies which are on low dividend yields reflecting their past and expected future good performance, oil companies, privatised utility stocks which have semi-monopoly positions and whose future profitability is affected by politically determined regulation, and other stocks. A similar exercise for each of these groups of companies could provide pointers to attractive investments, but such an exercise is outside the scope of this study.

It should be emphasised that the projections made in this chapter are for long-term movements in security prices and returns; the author makes no forecast of the change in the prices of equities during the next month or year. Nor would the author deny that the exercise reported here is open to Keynes's criticism that it 'assume[s] that the ... [post-1950 period] ... is a serviceable guide to the future'.

Data appendix

In this appendix the principal statistical series used in the preparation of the book are recorded. Although recent data for indices of share prices, etc. are readily available, series have to be linked to cover the period since 1926. The FT–Actuaries 500 Share Index was preferred to the All Share Index as the principal index because earnings data are not available for the latter.

Until the 1980s the best source of estimates of property values and yields was estimates prepared by firms of estate agents and, for consistency, series prepared by estate agents have been used for the whole of the period since 1967.

Equities (ordinary shares

The period 1926–63

Dividend yields
1926–63. Calculated by Moodies (LCES, 1971). Arithmetic average of yields of the equities included in their price index (50 equities were included for the period 1926–49, and 60 for the period 1950–63). Dividends are defined as the total of the latest year's dividends, up to the most recently declared, expressed as a percentage of total market capitalisation.

Share prices
1924–49. The London and Cambridge Economic Service (LCES) index for 92 industrial companies excluding finance and property companies. Annual figures are the arithmetic average of mid month prices.
1949–62. Moodies Services Ltd Index for 60 equities selected to represent the whole London market; excluding mines and plantations. The annual figures are *geometric* means of the prices quoted on Fridays.

Earnings yields

1927–63. A very rough series calculated by the LCES – the ratio of Moodies' indices of the percentage earned to the percentage paid on equities of 150 companies (1927–50: 50 companies) selected to represent the whole market excluding mines and plantations, lagged one year and multiplied by Moodies' dividend yield.

Period 1963–90

The source for the period 1963–90 was the FT–Actuaries 500 Share Index which represents industrial companies and excluding financial companies. Annual figures are arithmetic averages of those for working days.

Dividend yields

These are the totals of the last year's dividends, up to the most recently declared, payable on the capital of constituents expressed as percentages of total market capitalisation.

Earnings yield

Earnings are calculated from the latest available reports and accounts and interim statements and are expressed as percentages of total market valuation. Earnings are after tax, based on the assumption that there is maximum distribution of profits. Earnings are nominal profits before any adjustment for inflation. There was a break in the series in 1973 when the system of corporation tax was changed.

Prices

The price index used is the 'Consumers' expenditure average value index'. Sources: for 1926–48, LCES (1971) and for 1948–90, *Economic Trends*, various issues.

Property

The source for yields on shop properties was the agent Healey and Baker: the yields are representative of shops on prime sites. All the other series were obtained from the agents Jones, Lang and Wootton (JLW). Shop yields for the period 1967–70 were obtained from KMSO (1978, p. 152) and linked to the Healey and Baker series. For the period 1967 to 1976 the estimates of the capital values of shops are derived from the series of expected rental values for new lettings and yields on

Table A.1. *Equities and the money supply*

	Nominal share prices index	Dividend yield	Earnings yield	Index of consumer prices	Index of real share prices	Index of real dividends	Money supply M3 £bn
1926	100	6.17	(10.5)	100	100	100	2.27
7	107	5.46	9.3	97.1	110.2	97.5	2.3
8	123.3	5.00	8.8	96.8	127.4	103.2	2.34
9	120.8	5.47	8.9	95.7	126.2	111.9	2.38
1930	97.6	6.48	10.5	93.0	104.9	110.2	2.39
1	76.6	7.17	11.5	89.0	86.1	100.0	2.37
2	72.1	6.24	9.2	86.9	83.0	83.9	2.41
3	88.3	4.70	6.9	85.0	103.9	79.1	2.61
4	109.3	4.14	6.4	84.8	128.9	86.5	2.55
5	120.8	4.15	6.3	85.6	141.1	94.9	2.69
6	139.5	4.02	6.3	86.4	161.5	105.2	2.89
7	130.1	4.55	7.3	88.2	147.5	108.8	3.00
8	107	4.63	8.7	90.6	118.1	88.6	3.02
9	100	5.80	8.7	93.0	107.5	101.1	3.00
1940	81.3	6.19	11.8	108.9	74.7	74.9	3.29
1	88.3	5.52	9.4	120.3	73.4	65.7	3.80
2	97.6	4.76	8.1	128.3	76.1	58.7	4.28
3	116.3	4.09	7.0	132.9	87.5	58.0	4.90
4	127.8	3.89	7.3	135.6	94.2	59.4	5.56
5	134.8	3.74	6.8	139.3	96.8	58.7	6.29
6	146.5	3.60	6.8	144.4	101.5	59.2	6.81
7	153.5	4.08	7.9	154.8	99.2	65.6	7.54
8	148.8	4.61	9.9	166.6	89.3	66.7	7.66
9	139.5	5.05	12.9	170.8	81.7	66.8	7.73
1950	141.8	5.22	14.1	175.7	80.7	68.3	7.77
1	165.1	5.01	14.4	192.2	85.9	69.8	7.93
2	137.1	6.39	19.1	202.4	67.7	70.2	7.89
3	146.5	6.18	15.5	207.0	70.8	70.9	8.11
4	195.3	5.52	13.2	210.9	92.6	82.8	8.48
5	227.8	5.51	14.3	218.4	104.3	93.1	8.51
6	211.6	6.25	16.4	228.1	92.8	94.0	8.42
7	227.8	6.17	14.9	235.9	96.6	96.6	8.61
8	232.6	6.31	14.5	243.1	95.7	97.9	8.86
9	332.6	4.70	9.9	245.6	135.4	103.2	9.22
1960	420.9	4.29	9.3	248.3	169.5	117.9	9.56
1	434.9	4.77	9.6	255.6	170.1	131.5	9.86
2	409.3	5.09	9.6	265.1	154.4	127.4	10.08
3	462.8	4.40	7.7	269.7	171.6	122.4	10.5
4	493.7	4.63	8.1	279.4	176.7	132.6	11.1
5	464.5	5.54	8.0	293.1	158.5	142.3	11.9
6	468.5	5.67	7.7	304.8	153.7	141.3	12.6

Table A.1. (*cont.*)

	Nominal share prices index	Dividend yield	Earnings yield	Index of consumer prices	Index of real share prices	Index of real dividends	Money supply M3 £bn
7	500.2	5.16	6.9	312.7	160.0	133.8	13.3
8	707	3.69	4.9	327.7	215.7	129.0	14.6
9	698.8	3.90	5.8	345.9	202.0	127.7	15.1
1970	619.1	4.52	6.9	366.1	169.1	123.9	16.0
1	731.9	3.96	6.1	397.6	184.1	118.1	17.8
2	931.7	3.31	5.4	423.5	220.0	118.0	21.9
3	806.7	4.10	9.0	458.4	176.0	116.9	27.4
4	473.7	8.00	21.9	536.2	88.3	114.5	32.3
5	592.1	6.70	19.33	663.6	89.2	96.9	35.2
6	709.2	6.16	15.40	767.5	92.4	92.3	37.6
7	909.1	5.50	15.39	881.9	103.1	91.9	40.5
8	1024.4	5.48	16.15	962.8	106.4	94.5	46.5
9	1163.8	5.78	15.91	1093.8	106.4	99.7	52.5
1980	1243.8	6.59	19.00	1271.1	97.9	104.5	60.5
1	1402.6	5.96	14.64	1415.4	99.1	95.7	70.8
2	1625.3	5.47	12.34	1539.7	105.6	93.6	79.6
3	2051.6	4.60	10.12	1614.3	127.1	94.8	89.2
4	2440.3	4.46	10.56	1696.9	143.8	104.0	97.2
5	3012.9	4.38	10.38	1786.4	168.7	119.7	109.3
6	3738	3.93	9.15	1865.3	200.4	127.6	128.9
7	4572.2	3.41	7.64	1946.4	234.9	129.8	154.9
8	4439.7	4.25	10.01	2041.1	217.5	149.8	176.9
9	5319.0	4.12	9.81	2157.3	246.6	164.6	198.3
1990	5220.8	4.89	11.24	2265.0	230.5	182.7	216.3

Sources: See text.

shop properties (ERVs). In fact, capital values are related to actual rents as well as expected rents when a property is re-let.

Definitions

ERVs are the estimated rents for new lettings. They are based on rents negotiated for recent new leases. Net income is the actual income receivable on a portfolio of properties. It is net of any rents due to head landlords such as ground rents. Actual rents lag behind ERVs because current market rents only take effect when rents are renegotiated.

Over the period 1981 to 1990 the estimate of total returns on property investment made by JLW was closely in line with the average of estimates made by five agents.

Table A.2. Commercial property[a]

June	JLW[b] ERV[c]	JLW Net income	JLW capital	JLW return	Shops ERV[c]	Shops capital	Offices ERV[c]	Offices capital	Shops yields	Shops retail prices
1967	35	62	43	26	47	(41)	28		(6.25)	34
8	38	62	47	30	52	(48)	31		(6)	36
9	39	62	52	35	54	(52)	32		(5.75)	37
1970	44	62	56	39	59	(54)	36		(6)	40
1	52	59	65	48	60	(53)	47		6.25	43
2	60	78	74	57	69	(84)	55		4.25	46
3	71	79	95	76	83	(107)	68		4.25	51
4	86	80	77	66	97	(82)	85		6.50	59
5	95	83	77	70	99	(78)	95		7	74
6	99	90	86	81	100	(100)	99		5.50	85
7	100	100	100	100	100	100	100	100	5.50	100
8	108	117	121	127	115	126	103	115	4.50	107
9	124	129	145	160	131	155	118	136	4.25	120
1980	136	140	161	185	155	178	122	145	4	145
1	154	157	179	217	185	219	133	158	3.75	161
2	163	178	197	251	194	248	147	178	3.50	176
3	165	186	191	257	206	250	147	168	3.75	182
4	170	209	196	280	217	285	150	172	3.75	192
5	175	222	202	307	234	321	151	174	3.75	205
6	184	234	203	328	257	337	160	173	4	210
7	203	250	216	374	290	370	179	185	4	219
8	244	285	256	470	366	440	215	218	4	229
9	301	304	312	602	445	513	267	272	4.25	248
1990	338	384	331	637	483	486	301	276	5.25	272
1	333	433	273	599	484	438	286	234	5.50	288

Notes: [a] The figures in brackets are estimates. The method used to make the estimates and definitions of the terms are described in the text.
[b] Jones, Lang and Wootton. [c] Estimated rental values.
Source: The agents Jones, Lang and Wootton.

Notes

Introduction

1 The book value of a company's assets are the values given in the company's balance sheet.
2 Some customer business is direct between market makers and institutions and other investors, and the remainder is via brokers acting as agents for investors.
3 Source: UBS Phillips and Drew (1990, p. 19). Other groups of shareholders distinguished were charities (2%), industrial and commercial companies (4), government (5), overseas-based holders (8).
4 Estimates given by Moyle (1971) show the decline in the holdings of equities by persons from 1957. In 1957 they held 62% of UK equities; by 1970 their holdings had fallen to 45%. In the 1920s and 1930s personal holdings may have been substantially higher than two-thirds.

1 Keynes's explanation for the instability of share prices and investment

1 The main references are Lawson (1985, 1988, 1989, 1990), O'Donnell (1989), Dupuy (1989) and Runde (1990, 1991). No attempt is made in this chapter to assess the methodological arguments and implications which accompany these interpretations, although it is recognised that these are the central issues underlying the differing interpretations of chapter 12.
2 Short-term expectations concern decisions about what level of output to produce using existing capital equipment; such decisions turn on the expected production costs and sales proceeds of the chosen output and are short-term because they extend into the future only as far as it takes time to produce the output.
3 An interesting feature of Keynes's discussion in chapter 12, as Runde (1991) notes, is that despite being called 'The State of Long-term Expectations', it refers almost exclusively to expectations with relatively short-time horizons. This follows from the fact that the stock market offers individual investors the opportunity to 'get out' should they wish to do so. The need to form genuine long-term expectations thus becomes less urgent than in the case of investment in capital equipment.

4 In practice, there is a qualification to the link between share prices and investment in new assets which Keynes describes. If a company or an individual is to gain control of the assets of another company, the acquirer has to pay a premium to take over the company.

5 It is Keynes's stress on uncertainty in chapter 12 which has led some economists, including Shackle, to view it as the most important element of *The General Theory*. However, Shackle's interpretation has been questioned by, for example, O'Donnell (1989). He argued that Shackle's emphasis on uncertainty is one-sided; uncertainty is one central constituent of *The General Theory*, but so is the principle of effective demand and its equilibrating role in the operation of the system.

6 Contemporary investment analysts seem to have considerable confidence in their ability to forecast the future returns which will be derived from patent medicines (drugs) and even forecasts of returns from drugs which pharmaceutical firms will discover in the future. This confidence is indicated by the high prices of the shares of many pharmaceutical companies relative to the book value of their assets. The patent protection for drugs is more effective than patents on new products and product developments in most other industries.

7 Runde (1991) describes Keynes's conception of probability.

8 A noteworthy feature of this statement is that if an investor believes that the expected yield justifies a price of 30, but that the price will fall to 20, this assumes other investors assess the value of the share differently, that they will act perversely or that they will sell in the expectation of buying back at a lower price. Also the spread of prices quoted by Keynes is interesting: the price is expected to fall by 5 and then rise by 10 – if the expected fall is 1 or 2 and the rise 5 or 10 the decision may, of course, be different.

2   The Efficient Markets Hypothesis

1 See Baumol (1965).

2 For a discussion and critique of the underlying foundations of the rational expectations treatment of expectation formation and its incorporation of uncertainty into economic analysis, see Lawson (1988, 1990).

3 These theories have been developed by Bray (1989), Grossman and Stiglitz (1980) and Stiglitz (1982). See chapter 3 for a brief discussion of the Grossman and Stiglitz paper.

4 The possible reasons for, and effects of, investors inferring information from movements in prices are described in chapter 3.

5 Harry Roberts (1964) is usually credited with the original formulation of this statement.

6 The tendency in the subsequent empirical literature has been to take a purist's view of semi-strong efficiency and to adopt the position that if the information was in the public domain then it was available to the public and should be reflected in prices. This ignores the cost of acquiring information, but the intuitive justification for this position is that the costs of acquiring such public information are outweighed by the rewards.

3 Other explanations for the volatility of share prices

1 Similar theories based on the assumption of rational behaviour have been suggested to explain gambling, that gamblers take chances in an attempt to change their status (Brenner and Brenner, 1990).
2 Bulkley and Tonks (1989) claim to have isolated a 'trading rule' which would enable an investor to outperform the UK equity index. By switching from bonds to equities or vice versa on seven occasions from 1930 to 1985 they estimate returns would have been doubled in comparison to the return from their control portfolio with no trading. It is noteworthy that between 1971 and 1985 no switch was called for by the trading rule they identified – the hypothetical profitable trade took place earlier.
3 Romer (1990) reports a relationship between share prices, consumer confidence and expenditure on durables, particularly following the stock market crash in 1929.

4 The volatility of share prices

1 Kearns and Pagan (1990) use this indicator of volatility for their study of the volatility of Australian stock market prices.
2 References to the literature are given in chapter 2.
3 $\dfrac{\frac{1}{2}(137 - 87)}{\frac{1}{2}(137 + 87)} \times 100$
4 Risk Measurement Service, January–March 1991, p. 19.

5 The slow growth of real dividends

1 The sources of data for share prices and dividends are described in the Data appendix.
2 The sort of calculations made for this estimate are described in more detail in table 18.1.
3 Average share prices during the year changes of government took place have been used to make the 'political' comparisons. Share prices may change in advance of an election, anticipating the result, and there were movements of share prices before and after the elections in election years. The comparisons of dividends are not affected by movements of share prices.

7 The property market

1 The index of property values is compiled by the agents Jones, Lang and Wootton (JLW) 'to provide a yardstick ... to detect *general trends* in the property market'. *JLW Index Explanatory Notes*, July 1990, p. 4. The JLW Index was chosen for this chapter because it provides estimates of values since 1967. The sample of properties which were used to compile the Index had a value of £557m at March 1990. The Investment Property Databank (IPD) Index is based on a larger sample of properties than the JLW Index, but it provides information only for the period since 1980.
2 The benefits obtained from property developments are excluded from the

property index, but the effects of property development on share prices are not excluded from the index of share prices.

3 Both effects were uneven; some local authorities lost staff and had difficulty replacing them because of the high demand for planners from other local authorities and the private sector, and this slowed the response to planning applications. Shortages of components for some high tech building designs slowed this type of construction more than construction with traditional methods and materials.

8 The sample of institutions

1 Six further institutions which were approached declined to take part in the study.

9 The allocation of investments

1 At the end of 1989, 47% of the National Mutual's investment funds were in equities; it had 23% of its funds in fixed interest and a further 7% in variable rate mortgages.

2 A manager suggested that if they are given freedom, the forecasters would give wide ranges often centred around a return of 10%, but at an investment house which requires managers to make best estimates and ranges, the ranges did not centre on the best estimates in all cases.

3 If market indices are used to set targets, the FT–SE Index of 100 leading shares may be used for UK equity investment and an index for world equity markets such as the Morgan Stanley or FT–Actuaries Indices for overseas investments.

4 The reverse yield gap is the interest yield on bonds minus the dividend yield on equities.

10 Selection of shares

1 Heather Farmbrough (1990) has described the ambience in which a fund manager works.

2 For small companies these limits can be as low as, for example, 2,000 shares at 30p.

3 The house bought Austrian equities and shares of small Japanese companies for its clients in 1989. (Timing entry to small national markets such as Norway and Austria can be important. If and when such markets become fashionable for UK or American institutions there can be large price movements.)

4 Fund managers are not concerned with forecasting published profits alone. They have to assess the quality of the profits; for companies with overseas assets in, and earnings from less-developed countries, the accuracy and security of the earnings may be difficult to assess.

11 Market makers and views of the market

1 Market making was performed by jobbers before the Big Bang changes which are outlined in chapter 1.

2 Long positions occur when jobbers have bought more of a share than they have sold and short positions where they have sold more than they have bought. If a short position extends beyond an account the jobber has to borrow stock from a holder, usually an institution.

3 Abour 40% of turnover in UK equities on the stock exchanges is between market makers. Transactions between market makers are exempt from stamp duty.

4 Information about turnover in each share is published on a daily basis. Also, directors have an obligation to inform the Stock Exchange about their own transactions in their company's shares within three trading days and this information is published.

5 Agency brokers act as agents arranging for clients to buy from and sell to market makers, but not themselves make a market in shares.

6 Prior to Big Bang when jobbing and agency broking were separated, jobbers competed by setting prices for stocks but brokers charged fixed commissions.

12 Competition between fund managers and investment strategies

1 An institution can obtain substantial discounts on the initial charges when it buys units. If it buys at a time when a trust is facing a net withdrawal of funds it may be able to obtain units without an initial charge.

2 The advantage of general fund managers using options and not leaving their use to a specialist or specialist team is that decisions on options trading can be integrated with other portfolio decisions. If a manager is tempted to buy a stock but cannot do so without pushing the price up in front of his purchases, he may take an opportunity to write a put option.

3 In-house pension funds are funds managed by managers appointed by the company or trustees of the fund, not by independent managers.

14 The performance of fund managers

1 This issue of *Money Management* was selected as the most recent one available when the initial comparisons were made.

2 When funds are merged there are some loose rules for the treatment of the record for the pre-merger period. The treatment is usually decided by the Unit Trust Association and would follow the line 'as to which history is most relevant, establishing the suitability of the original fund objectives with the new'.

3 The fund had a 'high exposure to relatively small capitalisation, Midlands-based engineering and construction companies' and was 'best described as a recovery fund with a yield'.

4 It is conceivable that, if institutions do go liquid, the government may allow the money supply to rise and accommodate this demand for liquidity; *if* interest rates are higher than the return on equities (including capital appreciation) this could for a time increase the returns obtained by institutions.

17 Implications of the study

1 It was suggested to the author that unit trust managers do not offer such funds because they would not be popular with (a) some investors who want the *chance* of outperforming the indices and (b) agents selling the units because they would receive a lower commission if the initial charges were lowered.

2 Although a great many tests of the EMH have been made, an omission has been the comparison of the returns given of actual valuations of shares and the returns for hypothetical valuations over a period of, say, ten years. The hypothetical valuations could be based on asset value per share or current earnings or cash flow per share. The tests would show the extent to which actual valuations predict long-term performance compared to a mechanistic method of valuing shares and whether share valuations are as hit and miss as is claimed in this book. The tests were not made because the comparisons would require careful scrutiny of a large data base and resources were not available for this.

18 Are equities undervalued?

1 This chapter was written in September 1991.

2 $\dfrac{(104.62 \times 100.098)}{100} - 100$

3 The selection of shares is not based on net assets per share alone. Companies with high gearing ratios are avoided and shares in companies whose profits are expected to increase/recover are selected.

References

Ammer, J. M. (1990) Expenses, yields and excess returns; new evidence on closed end fund discounts, LSE Financial Markets Group Discussion Paper, London School of Economics

Anand, P. (1991) The nature of rational choice and the foundations of statistics, *Oxford Economic Papers*, vol. 43 no. 2, April

Argenti, J. (1984) *Predicting Corporate Failure*, London: Institute of Chartered Accountants in England and Wales

Bank of England (1987) Management of UK equity portfolios, *Bank of England Quarterly Bulletin*, vol. 27 no. 2, May

Baumol, W. J. (1965) *The Stock Market and Economic Efficiency*, New York: Fordham University Press

Bhagat, S., Shleifer, A. and Vishny, R. W. (1990) Hostile takeovers in the 1980s: the return to corporate specialization, *Brookings Paper on Economic Activity*, Special Issue on Microeconomics

Black, F. (1986) Noise, *Journal of Finance*, vol. 41 no. 3

Blanchard, O. J. and Watson, M. W. (1982) Bubbles, rational expectations and financial markets, in P. Wachtel (ed.), *Crisis in the Economic and Financial Structure*, Lexington, Mass.: Lexington Books

Bray, M. (1989) Rational expectations, information and asset markets, in F. Hahn (ed.), *The Economics of Missing Markets*, Oxford: Clarendon Press

Brealey, R. A. (1991) Harry M. Markowitz's contributions to financial economics, *Scandinavian Journal of Economics*, vol. 93 no. 1

Brenner, R. and Brenner, G. (1990) *Gambling and Speculation*, Cambridge: Cambridge University Press

Bulkley, G. and Tonks, I. (1989) Are UK stock prices excessively volatile?, *Economic Journal*, vol. 99 no. 398, December

BZW (1988) *BZW Equity-Gilt Study*, London: Barclays de Zoete Wedd

Capie, F. and Webber, A. (1985) *A Monetary History of the United Kingdom, 1870–1982*, London: Allen & Unwin

CAPS (1990) *Pension Fund Investment Performance*, Leeds: Combined Actuarial Performance Services

Cass, D. and Shell, K. (1983) Do sunspots matter?, *Journal of Political Economy*, vol. 91 no. 2

Cootner, P. H. (1964) *The Random Character of Stock Market Prices*, Cambridge, Mass.: MIT Press

Cowles, A. (1933) Can stock market forecasters forecast?, *Econometrica*, vol. 1 no. 4, July

Davis, E. P. (1990) An industrial approach to financial instability, Bank of England Discussion Papers no. 50, London

Debreu, G. (1959) *Theory of Value*, Newhaven: Yale University Press

Dimson, E. (1988) *Stock Market Anomalies*, Cambridge: Cambridge University Press

Dimson, E. and Marsh, P. (1982) Calculating the cost of capital, *Long Range Planning*, vol. 15 no. 2

Dupuy, J.-P. (1989) Common knowledge, common sense, *Theory and Decision*, vol. 27 no. 1

Earl, P. E. (1990) Economics and psychology: a survey, *Economic Journal*, vol. 100 no. 402, September

Eatwell, J., Milgate, M. and Newman, P. (1987) (eds.) *The New Palgrave: A Dictionary of Economics*, London: Macmillan

Economic Trends (various dates) London: Central Statistical Office

Eurostat (various dates) *Eurostat Review*, Brussels: Commission of the European Communities

Fama, E. (1970) Efficient capital markets: a review of theory and empirical work, *Journal of Finance*, vol. 25 no. 2

  (1976) *Foundations of Finance*, New York: Basic Books

  (1991) Efficient capital markets: II, *Journal of Finance*, vol. 46 no. 5

Fama, E. and Miller, M. (1972) *The Theory of Finance*, New York: Holt, Rinehart and Winston

Farrell, M. J. (1962) On the structure of the capital market, *Economic Journal*, vol. 72 no. 288, December

Farmbrough, H. (1990) 'Sorry, out to lunch', *Financial Times*, 29 December

Friedman, M. (1969) *The Optimum Quantity of Money*, London: Macmillan

Garber, P. (1990) Famous first bubbles, *Journal of Economic Perspectives*, vol. 4 no. 2

Goetzmann, W. N. and Ibbotson, R. G. (1990) Do winners repeat? Graduate School of Business, Columbia University Working Paper no. FB–91–04

Graham, B. and Dodd, D. L. (1934) *Security Analysis*, New York: McGraw-Hill

Granger, C. W. J. and Morgenstern, O. (1963) Spectral analysis of New York stock market prices, in Cootner, P. H. (1964)

Grossman, S. J. and Stiglitz, J. E. (1980) On the impossibility of informationally efficient markets, *American Economic Review*, vol. 70 no. 3

Gwilliam, D. and Russell, T. (1991) Polly Peck: where were the analysts?, *Accountancy*, January

Hamilton, J. (1986) On testing for self-fulfilling speculative bubbles, *International Economic Review*, vol. 27 no. 3

Hardouvelis, G. A. (1988) Evidence on stock market speculative bubbles: Japan, the United States, and Great Britain, *Federal Reserve Board of New York Quarterly Review*, Summer

Hayek, F. A. (1944) *The Road to Serfdom*, London: Routledge

HMSO (1978) *Evidence on the Financing of Industry and Trade*, Report of the Committee to review the functioning of financial institutions, London: HMSO

Hoare Govett (1990) *The Hoare Govett Smaller Companies Index 1990* (HG-SC), London: Hoare Govett

International Financial Statistics (various dates) *International Financial Statistics*, Washington, DC: International Monetary Fund

JLW (1988) *Property Index, Winter 1988*, London: Jones Lang and Wootton

Kaufman, H. (1986) *Interest Rates, the Markets and the New Financial World*, London: I. B. Tauris

Kearns, P. and Pagan, A. R. (1990) Australian stock market volatility: 1875–1987, University of Rochester Working Paper No. 248

Kendall, M. G. (1953) The analysis of economic time series. Part 1: prices, in Cootner, P. H. (1964)

Keynes, J. M. (1971–89) *The Collected Writings of J. M. Keynes*, (CW), edited by D. E. Moggridge, and E. Johnson, London: Macmillan (page references are to CW where a CW reprint is cited)

(1921) *A Treatise on Probability*, reprinted as vol. 8 of CW

(1936) *The General Theory of Employment, Interest and Money*, reprinted as vol. 7 of CW

(1937) The general theory of employment, *Quarterly Journal of Economics*, vol. 51, pp. 201–23, reprinted in vol. 14 of CW

(1939) Professor Tinbergen's method, *Economic Journal*, vol. 49, pp. 34–51, reprinted in vol. 14 of CW

(1983) Economic articles and correspondence: investment and editorial, vol. 12 of CW

Kindleberger, C. P. (1987) Bubbles, in Eatwell *et al.* (1987)

King, M. and Wadhwani, S. (1988) Transmission of volatility between stock markets, LSE Financial Group Working Paper No. 48, London School of Economics

Kupiec, P. (1991) Stock market volatility in OECD countries: recent trends, consequences for the real economy, and proposals for reform, OECD Economic Studies, No. 17

Lawson, T. (1985) Uncertainty and economic analysis, *Economic Journal*, vol. 95 no. 380, December

(1988) Probability and uncertainty in economic analysis, *Journal of Post Keynesian Economics*, vol. 11 no. 1

(1989) Abstraction, tendencies and stylised facts, *Cambridge Journal of Economics*, vol. 13 no. 1

(1990) Realism closed systems and expectations, paper given at the International School of Economic Research, Sienna

(1991) Keynes and rational behaviour, mimeo.

Lazar, D. (1990) *Markets and Ideology in the City of London*, London: Macmillan

LeRoy, S. F. (1989) Efficient capital markets and martingales, *Journal of Economic Literature*, vol. 27 no. 4, December

London and Cambridge Economic Service (LCES) (1971) *The British Economy: Key Statistics 1900–1970*, London: Times Newspapers

London Stock Exchange (various dates) *Quality of Markets Quarterly Review*, various issues

McInish, T. H. and Srivastava, R. K. (1984) The nature of individual investors' heterogeneous expectations, *Journal of Economic Psychology*, vol. 5, pp. 251–63

Macmillan, H. (1938) *The Middle Way*, London: Macmillan

Malkiel, B. G. (1985) *A Random Walk Down Wall Street*, London: Norton

M&G (various years) *M&G Yearbook*, various issues

Money Management (various dates) August

Moyle, J. (1971) *The Pattern of Ordinary Share Ownership 1957 to 1970*, Cambridge: Cambridge University Press

O'Donnell, R. M. (1989) *Keynes: Philosophy, Economics and Politics*, Basingstoke: Macmillan

Orléan, A. (1989) Mimetic contagion and speculative bubbles, *Theory and Decision*, nos. 1/2, July/September

Pesaran, M. H. (1989) On the volatility and efficiency of stock prices, DAE Working Paper No. 8908, Cambridge

Planned Savings (1990) *Planned Savings*, various issues.

Poterba, J. M. and Summers, L. H. (1987) Mean reversion in stock prices: evidence and implications, Harvard Institute of Economic Research, Discussion Paper 1349

Risk Measurement Service (various years) *Risk Measurement Service*, London: London Business School Financial Services

Roberts, H. V. (1964) Stock-market 'patterns' and financial analysis: methodological suggestions, in Cootner, P. H. (1964)

Romer, C. D. (1990) The great crash and the onset of the great depression, *Quarterly Journal of Economics*, vol. 105 no. 3

Ross, S. (1987) Finance, in Eatwell *et al.* (1987)

Runde, J. (1990) Keynesian uncertainty and the weight of arguments, *Journal of Economics and Philosophy*, vol. 6 no. 2

(1991) Keynesian uncertainty and the instability of beliefs, *Review of Political Economy*, vol. 3 no. 2

(1992) Keynesian uncertainty and liquidity preference, mimeo.

Samuelson, P. A. (1965) Proof that properly anticipated prices fluctuate randomly, *Industrial Management Review*, vol. 6, pp. 41–49

Sen, A. K. (1985) Rationality and uncertainty, *Theory and Decision*, vol. 18, pp. 109–127

(1987) Rational behaviour, in Eatwell *et al.* (1987)

Seyhun, H. N. (1990) Over-reaction or fundamentals ..., *Journal of Finance*, vol. 45 no. 5

Shackle, G. L. S. (1967) *The Years of High Theory, 1926–39*, Cambridge: Cambridge University Press

Shiller, R. J. (1981) Do stock prices move too much to be justified by subsequent changes in dividends?, *American Economic Review*, vol. 71 no. 3, June

(1989) *Market Volatility*, Cambridge, Mass. and London: MIT Press

Statistical Year Book of Japan (various dates)

Simon, H. A. (1982) *Models of Bounded Rationality*, Cambridge, Mass.: MIT Press

Stiglitz, J. E. (1982) Information and capital markets, in W. F. Sharpe and C. M. Cootner (eds.), *Financial Economics: Essays in Honour of Paul Cootner*, London: Prentice Hall

(1990) Symposium on bubbles, *Journal of Economic Perspectives*, vol. 4 no. 2

Tobin, J. (1984) On the efficiency of the financial system, *Lloyds Bank Review*, July, no. 153

UBS Phillips and Drew (1990) *UK Equity Market Indicators August 1990*, London, New York, Tokyo and Zurich: UBS Phillips and Drew

Unit Trust Year Book (various dates) London: Financial Times Business Information

Vercelli, A. (1991) *Methodological Foundations of Macroeconomics: Keynes and Lucas*, Cambridge: Cambridge University Press

Vickers, D. (1978) *Financial Markets in the Capitalist Process*, Philadelphia: University of Pennsylvania Press

Walras, L. (1954) *Elements of Pure Economics*, New York: Augustus M. Kelley

Wihlborg, C. (1990) The incentive to acquire information and financial market efficiency, *Journal of Economic Behavior and Organisation*, vol. 13 no. 3

WM Company (1990) *WM UK Pension Fund Service Annual Review 1989*, London, Edinburgh, Amsterdam and New York: The World Marketing Company

Working, H. (1934) A random difference series for use in the analysis of time series, *Journal of the American Statistical Association*, vol. 29 no. 185

Index